# Sinfully Yours
## Just Desserts

Foreword
Rashmi Uday Singh

Om Books International

First published in 2024 by

**Om Books International**

Corporate & Editorial Office
A-12, Sector 64, Noida 201 301
Uttar Pradesh, India
Phone: +91 120 477 4100
Email: editorial@ombooks.com
Website: www.ombooksinternational.com

Sales Office
107, Ansari Road, Darya Ganj, New Delhi 110 002, India
Phone: +91 11 4000 9000
Email: sales@ombooks.com
Website: www.ombooks.com



Cover Photo: Dabboo Ratnani



ISBN: 978-81-960433-4-6

Printed in India

10 9 8 7 6 5 4 3 2 1

# Contents


Foreword ..... 4–5

Classic Desserts ..... 6–43

1 Chocolate Walnut Cake
2 Chocolate Cookies
3 Lemon Semifreddo
4 Pavlova
5 Devil's Dark Fantasy
6 Eggless Choco Fudge
7 Fruit Trifle
8 Eggless Low-Fat Tutti Frutti Cake
9 Tiramisu
10 Salt Caramel Custard
11 Oats Cupcakes
12 Berry Panna Cotta
13 EgglessCaramel Custard
14 Matcha Tea Cake
15 Lemon Tart
16 Plum Cake
17 Eggless Chocolate Chip Cookies
18 Walnut and Fig Pie
19 My Fudgy Brownies
20 Cinnamon and Oats Tea Cake
21 Coconut Macaroons

Indian Delicacies ..... 44–69

22 Gulab Jamun with Jaggery
23 Seviyan Kheer
24 Lauki Halwa
25 Moong Dal Halwa
26 Puran Poli
27 Modak
28 Peanut Chikki
29 Kaju Katli
30 Fruit Jalebi
31 Payasam
32 Rabri Malpua
33 Mango Shrikhand
34 Sitaphal Rabri
35 Papaya Halwa

Quickie Desserts ..... 70–85

36 Peanut Butter Cups
37 1 Minute Microwave Eggless Brownie
38 Mocha Truffles
39 Peanut Butter Cupcakes
40 Mango Ice Cream
41 Dry Fruit Laddoos
42 Crepes
43 Healthy Bite on the Go!
44 Banoffee Split
45 Coconut Laddoos
46 Microwave Banana Pudding

Indian Fusion Desserts ..... 86–161

47 Makhana Pudding
48 Rava Cake
49 Pineapple Sandesh
50 Custard Bites
51 Pineapple Sheera
52 Beetroot Halwa
53 Baked Chilli Yogurt
54 No-Bake Choco-Walnut Tarts
55 Chocolate Duo Mousse
56 Strawberry Banana Coconut Pop
57 Banana Berry Fruit
58 Mango Coconut Frozen Yogurt
59 Chocolate Fudge
60 Chocolate Coconut Balls
61 Peanut Butter Fudge
62 3-Ingredient Nutella Brownie
63 Peach Crumble
64 French Hot Chocolate
65 Baked Custard
66 Marble Cake
67 Easy Chocolate Chip Mug Cake
68 Simple Choco Chip Cookies
69 Bread and Butter Pudding
70 My Delicious Scones
71 Banana Bread
72 Apple Cake
73 Eggless Banana Sponge
74 Mini Salted Caramel Tarts
75 Peanut Butter Cups
76 Almond Cake
77 Banana Muffins
78 Date Loaf
79 Coffee Cake
80 Assorted Donuts
81 Cranberry and Almond Muffins
82 Chocolate Date Nut Bars
83 Vanilla Banana Ice Cream
84 Flourless Sweet Potato Brownies
85 Energy Bites
86 Fresh Fruit Frozen Yogurt
87 5-Ingredient Healthy Brownies
88 Oats Truffles
89 Banana and Cinnamon Ice Cream
90 Oats Crepes
91 Coconut Flour Pancake
92 Almond and Date Bites
93 Amaranth Kheer with Nuts and Berries
94 Almond Flour Chocolate Cake
95 Almond and Saffron Phirni
96 Vegan Kheer
97 Hazelnut Butter Truffles
98 Ragi Kheer
99 Gluten-Free Porridge with Goji Berries and Mixed seed

Gluten-Free Desserts ..... 162–187

100 Strawberry Cheesecake Vegan Bars
101 Topping Berry Compote
102 No-Cream Caramel Sauce
103 Sugar Cookies
104 Vegan and Gluten-Free Donuts
105 Gluten-Free Marble Cake
106 Carrot Cake
107 Apple Cinnamon Crepes
108 Chocolate Bars (Vegan)
109 S'Mores
110 Chocolate Pie
111 Cherry Pie
112 Gluten-Free Pumpkin Bars
113 Snickerdoodle Peanut Butter Cookies
114 Gluten-Free Ragi Cupcakes

Vegan Desserts ..... 188–211

115 Vegan Chocolate Sesame Cookies
116 Vegan Hot Chocolate
117 Vegan Fudge
118 Vegan Pancake
119 Vegan Cheesecake
120 Pomegranate and Gingerbread Cake
121 Vegan Rabri
122 Vegan Rum Cake
123 Guava Ice Cream
124 Vegan Panna Cotta
125 Vegan Cinnamon Rolls
126 Vegan Cherry and Almond Brownies
127 Pecan Pie Bars
128 Blueberry Millet Tarts
129 Vegan Chocolate Avocado Mousse

Acknowledgements ..... 212

Index .... 214

# Foreword

Here it is. The ultimate sinfully virtuous sweet seduction! It gives me immense joy to write the foreword to *Sinfully Yours: Just Desserts*. After all, this unique collection of recipes is created, innovated and shared by the gorgeous, multi-talented queen of cuisine herself. Shipra Khanna is as glamorous as she is disciplined, as international as she is Hindustani, as much a sweet addict as she is into health and fitness. And it is this masterly balance that infuses this unique collection of recipes with its flavour.

Over the years I've had the good fortune to not only introduce her and be part of a round-table discussion with her in Spain, to taste her masterpieces but also have a first-hand experience of the adulation she inspires around the world. It is in Bilbao, the capital city of Basque, the gourmet capital of Spain that I am thrilled to witness great amount of interest and excitement about Indian cuisine. It's making waves on prime-time television news, newspaper and magazine articles, et al.

At the centre of it is our very own long-legged beautiful Shipra Khanna, an internationally acclaimed master chef, TV host, award-winning author, philanthropist, and content creator with a digital presence of over 50 million followers. She is making waves with her global fame by being the only Indian to be honoured as 'Celebrity Chef Influencer' at the WIBA awards at the Cannes Festival. Talk of making India proud! She cooks up multi-course menus in the most prestigious of venues. Shipra dresses in the most elegant and stylish way – she is as much a style icon as a culinary one. I admire her because she is a brilliant combination of both style and substance. A powerful and potent combination indeed. Sure enough, her strong digital presence is impressive but what is truly inspirational is that she did not let her abusive marriage weigh her down and went on to become a culinary queen. Showered with countless awards and accolades, she continues to be down to earth, humble and great fun to be with. That she has honed and refined her culinary expertise over the years is quite evident in the master chef's prowess, award-winning cookbooks, YouTube channels and TV shows.

I'm convinced the world is divided into two kinds of people: those who love the sweet stuff and those who don't. Here's the ultimate sweet offering which will surely dazzle sweet-addicts. You don't have a sweet tooth? This cookbook is guaranteed to convert you. Several good reasons unfold as you will read on. It is sinfully over the top, flamboyant, but has a backbone of deep research. A rigorous discipline infuses the collection and it spans the entire range – classics, Western and Indian, fusion, healthy and vegan recipes. Inspired by Shipra's grandmother (who brought her up), this cookbook took her a year-and-a-half to complete after several trials and testing by her family, cousins, nephews and nieces.

What you are holding in your hands is as gorgeous as it is sinfully seductive and masterfully constructed. As many as 129 recipes span the entire spectrum from the decadent and over-the-top flamboyant to the vegan and healthy. From the complex to the quickies, from all parts of the globe to *Dil hai Hindustani* too. From simple microwave brownies to healthy millet Christmas cake; from classics to her fusion recipes and more. Each recipe is tried, tasted, and tested.
Cook from the book, feast on the anecdotes from Shipra's childhood, her personal preferences, tips and secrets ... all shared in a candid and riveting style. What are you waiting for? Turn the pages and enjoy!

**Rashmi Uday Singh**
Indian Food Critic, Author and TV Host

# Classic Desserts

**Classic Desserts** always take me back to when I first discovered my love for baking. The simple yet rich perfection of my mother's Chocolate Cake. The refreshing citrus sweetness of a Lemon Tart in summer. The golden gorgeousness of a jiggly Caramel Custard sitting soaked in its own pool of syrup. My first magical bite of Macaroons with their immaculately baked outer shells and the most divine fillings inside. Or the creamy, coffee-tinted explosion of flavours in a classic Tiramisu.

These all-time favourites are what mesmerized both my thoughts and my taste buds and prompted me to know more about what went into making them and how they were prepared. And this is one love affair that has only grown deeper with time.

Some people might call Classic Desserts old-school but I simply adore their timeless appeal. I also believe that every baker must first understand and practise the classics, before they move on to more experimental or fancy baking. Classics lay a firm foundation stone for learning and honing the finer nuances of baking Classic Desserts perfectly. In fact, they have made a significant difference to both my skills and knowledge as a baker.

For me the smell of baking is as intoxicating as the taste of the final products and Classic Desserts are the most satisfying way to fill your home with that addictive and unmatchable fragrance of baking. Imagine warm, freshly baked Cookies, straight out of the oven or the Yuletide cheer you can smell when a rich Fruit Cake is baked – the classic recipes surely deliver in more delicious ways than one!

In this section, I have shared my favourite classic recipes and I hope they become your favourites too and get passed down through generations. Just dive in and bake that decadent Devil's Dark Fantasy Chocolate Cake that you always loved but never dared to try. Whisk up that perfectly crisp yet gooey-on-the-inside Pavlova that you have only admired on food magazine covers before this. I have also added my own twists to certain recipes, so there is a Matcha Tea Cake recipe and Lemon Semifreddo that I hope will add some contemporary charm to the vintage classics, while still retaining their timeless appeal.

Now pick your favourite Classic Dessert recipe and get started on whipping up something that everyone, including you, will fall in love with! Wishing you joy and happy learning in your baking journey and much deliciousness!

# Chocolate Walnut Cake

Here is a classic recipe that you cannot go wrong with. Chocolate walnut cakes are a classic that are liked by everyone across all cultures and age groups. Easy to bake, and even easier to gorge in. Any time you feel like having some chocolaty goodness, you can get whipping for supreme flavours!

## Ingredients

2 eggs
½ cup olive oil
½ cup chopped walnuts
½ cup chocolate chips
¾ cup all-purpose flour
¾ cup white caster sugar, powdered
¼ cup unsweetened cocoa powder
1 tsp baking powder
1 tsp vanilla extract
¼ tsp salt

## Method

- Sift the flour and cocoa powder in a bowl. Add baking powder, salt and sugar and whisk well.
- Next add eggs, oil and vanilla extract and whisk till well blended.
- Now add walnuts and choco chips.
- Prepare a 7.5-inch loaf pan by greasing with oil and keep baking paper at the bottom of the pan.
- Pour the cake batter into the prepared cake pan. Shake the pan to let the batter settle and be free from the air bubbles.
- Bake in the centre of an oven preheated to 180°C (355°F) for 40–45 minutes, till a skewer inserted in the cake comes out clean.
- Turn the cake onto a cooling rack until it cools down completely. Slice and serve.

# 2 Chocolate Cookies

This is the smaller, less guilty version of a chocolate walnut cake. Instead of gobbling up the whole cake, you can pick one or two cookies at a time (if you can restrain yourself, that is). You can get together with your family and make this a family activity on a weekend, where you come together and create chocolate cookies for the week!

## Ingredients

- 100 gm butter (softened)
- 1¼ cup flour
- 1 cup powdered sugar
- 1 tsp vanilla extract
- ½ tsp baking powder
- ¼ cup cocoa powder
- Pinch of salt
- 1½ cup sand, for baking in cooker

- Sift plain flour, cocoa powder, baking powder and pinch of salt in a bowl.
- Mix butter, powdered sugar and vanilla extract in another bowl and beat until well blended. Fold in the flour mix to make a smooth dough. Form a soft dough making sure not to knead.
- To prepare the cookies in a pressure cooker add sand in the cooker, put a cooker rack and place a plate above it. Close the lid of the cooker without the gasket and whistle. Heat it for 5–10 minutes on high flame. Now, shape the cookies by putting in least possible pressure. Put the shaped cookies on the plate. Cover and cook on medium flame for 15–17 minutes, till a skewer inserted into the centre of a cookie comes out clean. Cool and store it for a week in an airtight container.

3

## Ingredients

**For the candied lemon zest**

4 lemon (zest)

1 cup sugar

1 cup cold water

**For the lemon curd**

½ cup fresh lemon juice

1 cup jaggery

1 egg

4 egg yolks

½ cup butter

2 ½ cups chilled cream

Juice of 1 lemon

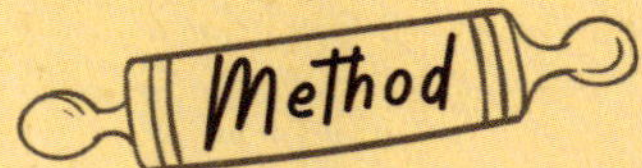


- Remove the zest from the lemons with a zester.
- Ensure that you do not add any of the bitter white pith.
- Place the zest in a small bowl, add boiling water, and let it stand.
- Drain after 30 minutes.
- Bring the sugar and water to a boil in a small saucepan over medium-high heat, keep stirring to dissolve.
- Add the zest, reduce the heat to medium-low, and cook for 10 minutes. Transfer the zest and syrup to a bowl, cover and keep aside.
- In a bowl take lemon juice, jaggery, egg, egg yolks and butter and whisk them together. Transfer the mixture in a large heavy saucepan and cook over medium heat, whisking constantly, until it begins to boil and becomes thick and pudding-like; it may take 10 to 15 minutes. Strain the curd through a fine-mesh strainer into a bowl, and set the bowl in the ice bath. Stir the curd periodically until it is cool, then remove the bowl from the ice bath and place a sheet of plastic wrap directly on the

surface of the lemon curd. Refrigerate for at least 1 hour.

- Whip 1½ cups of the chilled whipping cream in a large mixing bowl with a wire, whisk until soft peaks form. Remove the chilled lemon curd from the refrigerator, and set ½ cup aside for the sauce. Gently fold the remaining lemon curd into the whipped cream until well combined to create a soft lemon mousse.
- Cover and transfer to the freezer to firm up for at least 4 hours.
- Drain the candied lemon zest, reserving the syrup for the sauce, and set the zest aside on a plate or sheet of parchment. Whisk ⅓ cup of the lemon syrup with the remaining ½ cup lemon curd and the lemon juice in a small bowl; set the sauce aside.
- Meanwhile, whisk the remaining 1 cup chilled cream in a medium bowl until soft peaks form. Unmould the mousse onto individual dessert plates. Spoon the lemon sauce around the mousse, top it with whipped cream, and finish with a garnish of candied lemon zest and some crumble.

4

# Pavlova

## Ingredients

- 4 large egg whites (room temperature)
- 1 cup plus 2 tbsp superfine sugar
- 1 tsp corn starch
- 1 tsp vinegar
- 1 tsp pure vanilla extract
- 1¼ cups heavy cream, whipped
- Pinch of salt
- 10 passion fruits, for serving
- 4 bananas, for serving
- Mixed berries, such as raspberries, blueberries, strawberries, boysenberries, or blackberries, for serving

## Method

- Preheat oven to 300°F or 150°C.
- Using an 8-inch bowl as a guide, trace the perimeter of the bowl on to a sheet of parchment paper. Transfer parchment paper, pencil side down, to a baking sheet. Set aside.
- In the bowl of an electric mixer fitted with the whisk attachment, beat egg whites and salt together until glossy peaks form. With mixer running, add sugar in three additions, beating until meringue is stiff and glossy.
- Sprinkle in corn starch, vinegar, and vanilla; gently fold to combine.
- Mound the meringue in the centre of the 8-inch circle. Using a spatula, evenly spread meringue out towards the edges.
- Transfer baking sheet to oven and immediately reduce the temperature to 250°F or 120°C. Bake for 1 hour and 15 minutes.
- Turn off the oven and let meringue cool completely. When meringue is cool and completely dry, top it up with whipped cream and desired fruits.

CAKE

5

# Devil's Dark Fantasy

## Ingredients

**Batter**

½ cup almond flour
1 cup cocoa powder
1 tsp baking powder
½ tsp soda
1 cup caster sugar
3 eggs
1 cup butter
1 tsp vanilla extract
½ cup milk

**Ganache**

½ cup cream
1 cup choco chips

## Method

**Batter**

- Sift the flour, cocoa powder, baking powder and soda into a bowl. Whisk the sugar and eggs in another bowl till light and fluffy. Add butter and vanilla extract in the sugar–egg mixture and whisk till combined. Spoon the batter into a lightly greased cake mould.
- Bake in an oven preheated at 150°C or 300°F for 40–45 minutes, till a skewer inserted in the centre of the cake comes out clean. Turn the cake out on to a wire rack to cool completely.

**Ganache**

- Warm the cream in a pan on low heat. Add the choco chips, cover and set aside for 5 minutes. Mix till smooth and well blended. Refrigerate for 30 minutes.
- Slice the cake horizontally in half. Cover one half with ganache. Put the second half over the ganache. Spread the remaining ganache over the top and sides of the cake. Refrigerate and serve chilled.

6
Eggless Choco Fudge
Ingredients
½ cup flour
1 cup cocoa powder
1 tsp baking powder
1 tsp baking soda
½ cup yogurt
½ cup condensed milk
3 tbsp milk
1 cup demerara sugar
150 gm butter, at room temperature
A few drops of vanilla extract
Milk

- Sift the flour, cocoa powder, baking powder and baking soda in a bowl. Whisk the yogurt, condensed milk, sugar and milk in another bowl, till well blended. Add the butter and mix, till well combined. Fold in the flour mix, to make a smooth batter. Mix the vanilla extract.

- Spoon the batter into an 8-inch cake mould lined with butter paper. Bake in the centre of an oven preheated to 180°C or 355°F for 30–45 minutes, till a skewer inserted comes out clean. Turn the cake out on to a wire rack to cool. Slice and serve.

# 7 Fruit Trifle

Inspired by the English cuisine, this is an easy method of making the very famous and very delicious Trifle. All you need to do is assemble the ingredients, and voila! You are ready to create an aesthetically pleasing dessert that will win the hearts of your loved ones instantly!

## Ingredients

- 500 gm thick vanilla custard
- 500 ml thickened cream, whipped
- 250 gm sponge cake
- 1 cup jelly, prepared
- Fruits of your choice

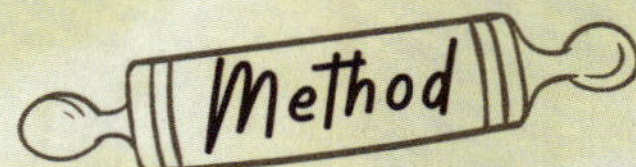

## Method

- Place a single layer of sponge cake around the base and sides of a 2½-litre serving dish.
- Make an even layer of jelly over the base. Pour custard over the jelly and spread evenly. Cover the custard layer with whipped cream.
- Decorate with fruits. Refrigerate until ready to serve.

8

# Eggless Low-Fat Tutti Frutti Cake

Do you know what is the most delightful thing about a tutti frutti cake? The chunks of tutti frutti that you look for as you bite into the cake becomes a little like a treasure hunt, trying to find the delicious bits of candy in the heavenly cake. So why not create your own treasure hunt as you bake a tutti frutti cake of your own?

## Ingredients

- 1½ cup plain flour
- ¾ cup curd
- ¾ cup sugar
- ¼ cup water
- ¼ cup tutti frutti
- ½ tsp baking soda
- ½ cup olive oil
- 1 tsp vanilla extract
- 1 tsp baking powder

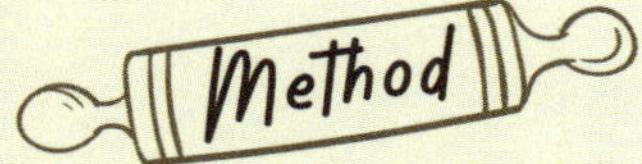


- Take curd, sugar, oil, vanilla extract in a bowl and whisk well. Sift plain flour, baking soda and baking powder into the same. Mix it well. Add water and make a thick, flowing-consistency batter. Add tutti frutti into it and mix well.
- Grease a cake mould with butter and keep a butter paper in the same. Transfer the cake batter in it. Bake in the centre of an oven preheated to 180°C or 355°F for 30–40 minutes, till a toothpick or a skewer inserted in the cake comes out clean.
- Serve or store in an airtight container.

9

# Tiramisu

## Ingredients

**Coffee cream**

1 tbsp coffee, dissolved in 2 tbsp water
1 tbsp rum (optional)
1 cup whipped cream

**To assemble**

6 slices vanilla sponge cake
Coffee cream
2 tbsp cocoa powder
100 gm chocolate shavings

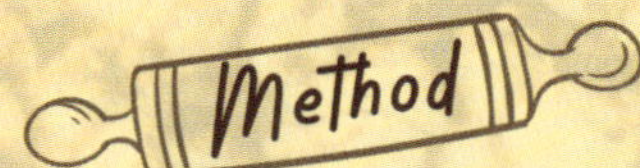

## Method

- Mix the coffee with water and rum in a bowl. Add it to the whipped cream in another bowl and mix well. Let it chill in the refrigerator for an hour.
- Dip the vanilla sponge cake in the dissolved coffee. Arrange 3 slices of sponge cake in a transparent glass bowl. Cover with the coffee cream.
- Put the remaining slices of cake on top. Cover with the coffee cream. Dust with cocoa powder. Chill in the refrigerator for an hour, decorate with chocolate shavings and serve.

10

## Ingredients

**Caramel**
1 tbsp water
1 cup sugar
2 tsp butter

**Custard**
1 cup milk
1 cup cream
3 tbsp sugar
2 egg yolks
A few drops of vanilla extract

**Topping**
Rock salt

**Caramel**

- Put the water and sugar in a heavy-based pan over medium heat till the sugar melts completely and is caramelized.
- Remove from heat, add butter and stir carefully and pour 1 tbsp each into 4–5 small ramekins.

**Custard**

- Put the milk, cream and sugar in a pan on low heat and stir till the sugar dissolves.
- Remove from heat and whisk the eggs and vanilla extract into the milk and cream. Pour the custard over the caramel in the ramekins. Cover the ramekins tightly with foil. Place them in a large baking tray filled with hot water up to one inch.
- Transfer the tray to an oven preheated to 180°C or 355°F and bake for 45–50 minutes, till the custard is set. Cool and chill in the refrigerator. Turn the custard out on to individual dessert plates, drizzle salt on top and serve.

# 11 Oats Cupcakes

Ah, cupcakes! With icing, without icing, cupcakes are the mini, cuter version of cakes and for the most part can help you remain guilt-free (relatively). Here is my way of creating mini cakes for you guys. Hope you try them out!

## Ingredients

1¼ cups ground oats flour
¾ cup fresh curd
¼ cup water
¼ cup olive oil
½ cup sugar (powdered)
1 tsp vanilla extract
1 tsp baking powder
½ tsp baking soda
Pinch of salt
Chopped nuts
6 cupcake moulds

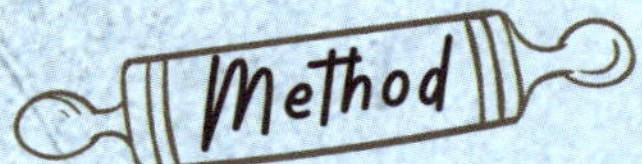

## Method

- In a mixing bowl, take curd, oil and vanilla extract and whisk until the oil and curd are well combined.
- Now sift flour, powdered sugar, baking powder, baking soda and a pinch of salt. Whisk and combine. Add water and make a smooth batter. Add chocolate chips and fold gently.
- Grease the cupcake moulds lightly. Spoon the batter into cupcake moulds. Roughly spread a few chopped nuts over the cupcake batter.
- Bake in the centre of an oven preheated to 180°C or 355°F for 15 minutes. Cool down the cakes completely and serve.

12

# Berry Panna Cotta

## Ingredients

200 gm coconut cream
1 tsp vanilla extract
2 tsp gelatin, dissolved in 2 tbsp warm water
100 ml buttermilk

**Sauce**

200 gm blueberries
25 gm sugar
1 cinnamon stick

**Decoration**

300 gm mixed berries (mulberry, blueberry, raspberry)

## Method

- Put the cream in a pan on low heat and bring it to a boil. Remove and stir in the vanilla extract. Strain in the dissolved gelatin and stir for about 1 minute.
- Mix in the buttermilk. Spoon into 11–12 greased 3-inch wide ramekins and refrigerate for 3–4 hours till it sets and the panna cotta leaves the sides of the dish.
- Combine the sauce ingredients in a pan and boil on medium heat till the blueberries soften and it has a syrupy consistency. Mash the blueberries in the sauce and strain. Chill it in the refrigerator.
- Turn out the panna cotta on to individual dessert plates. Spoon the blueberry sauce and add fresh berries on top and serve.

# Eggless Caramel Custard

## Ingredients

- ¼ cup sugar, caramelised
- ½ cup milk
- ½ cup cream
- ½ cup condensed milk
- 1 tbsp custard powder, vanilla flavoured
- 1 tsp vanilla extract

There is an easy yet promising way of making a classy dessert like a caramel custard. Honestly, no one hates the flavour, and it is a common favourite among the kids. You can add whichever fruits you like in the custard to add to the dish but caramel custard is in itself a delicious dessert to be devoured.

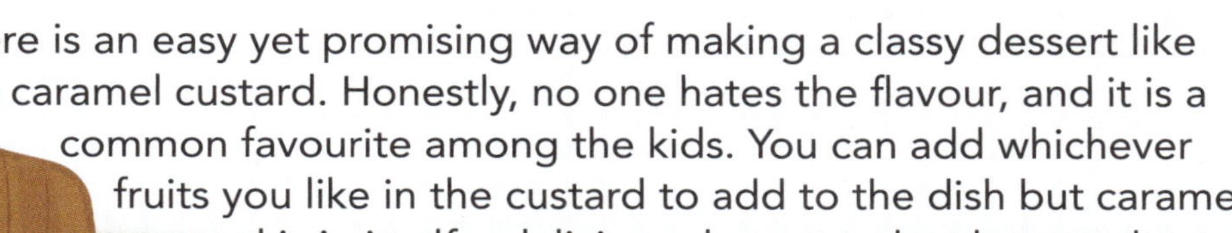

## Method

- Apply the caramelised sugar into a bowl and let it set completely.
- In another large bowl take milk, cream, condensed milk, custard powder and vanilla extract. Whisk and mix until everything is well combined. Pour in the bowl in which caramelized sugar is set.
- Cover and steam for about 30 minutes. Let it cool down to room temperature and then refrigerate. After 2 hours unmould the caramel custard and enjoy.

# 14 Matcha Tea Cake

Sometimes all you want to do is sit with your friends, and enjoy a high tea of your own. This tea cake is for the days when you are craving that moment for yourself! Easy to bake and oh, so delicious! It will have you dreaming about tea cakes for days after you are done baking it!

## Ingredients

2 eggs
1 cup flour
1 tbsp matcha powder
1 tsp baking powder
½ tsp baking soda
¾ cup cream
¾ cup brown sugar
1 tsp ground cinnamon
1 tsp icing sugar

## Method

- In a bowl take eggs, cream, sugar and beat well. Add flour while beating the batter. Now add matcha powder and fold it gently. Transfer in a pre-greased 8-inch cake mould.
- Bake for 30–40 minutes. Cover it with icing sugar and cinnamon. Let it cool at room temperature and serve.

15

# Lemon Tart

Who doesn't like the tangy taste of a lemon? Personally, I love it when citrus fruit is combined with creamy and indulgent flavours. Here is a recipe of Lemon Tart, something I know you will definitely enjoy!

## Method

- In a bowl, take sugar, lemon juice, cream and rind and whip together. Add eggs one by one and beat.
- Prepare the tart base and let it cool down at room temperature. Pour the batter in it and bake for 20–25 minutes in a moderate oven. Let it cool at room temperature. Serve.

## Ingredients

3 eggs
⅓ cup caster sugar
⅓ cup lemon juice
¼ cup thick cream
Few tart shells (see recipe of making tarts in recipe no. 74)
2 tsp lemon rind grated

# 16 Plum Cake

There is only one word that is synonymous with plum cake – Christmas! The joy of baking comes to fruition only when you can see your loved ones – your family and friends enjoy what you have created from scratch. Christmas is an occasion where the family gets together and celebrates with as much joy as any other festival. To make the most of it, here is a Plum Cake recipe that you can win hearts with!

## Ingredients

¼ cup raisins, finely chopped
¼ cup cranberries, finely chopped
¼ cup figs, finely chopped
¼ cup cherries, finely chopped
¼ cup apricot, finely chopped
¼ cup pitted dry dates, finely chopped
1 cup orange juice

**For the batter**

2 cups plain flour
1¼ cups water, warm
1 cup brown sugar (powdered)
¾ cup olive oil
1 tsp baking powder
1 tsp vanilla extract
½ tsp baking soda
½ tsp cinnamon powder
½ tsp orange zest
¼ tsp almonds, finely chopped
¼ tsp nutmeg powder
¼ tsp walnuts

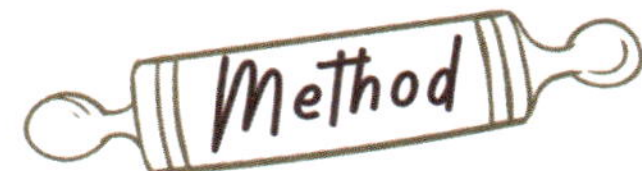


## Method

- Soak the dry fruits in orange juice for two days.
- Then take warm water, sugar, oil, and blend it well. In a bowl, sift plain flour, baking powder, baking soda, cinnamon powder, nutmeg powder, cardamom powder and salt followed by orange zest and vanilla extract.
- Blend till the batter is well combined, add dry fruits and put them into the batter. Mix well gently.
- Transfer the cake batter into the cake mould. Bake at 180°C or 355°F for 40–45 minutes. Garnish with walnuts, almonds and serve.

17

# Eggless Chocolate Chip Cookies

Cookies are almost everyone's favourite! And they are even more special when they are chocolate chip cookies. I have been making this for years and everyone who has tried these came back with amazing feedbacks. So now I am sharing this recipe with you, I hope you will love it too

## Ingredients

2 cup chocolate chips
1 cup plain flour
1 cup butter, melted
1 cup chopped walnuts
¾ cup brown sugar
¾ cup granulated sugar
1 tsp baking soda
1 tsp vanilla extract
½ tsp salt

## Method

- Sift flour in a bowl, add baking soda and salt. Mix and set aside. In a large bowl, take softened butter, vanilla and sugar. Beat together until fluffy. Mix well.
- Then gradually add flour. Once the dough is ready, add chocolate chips followed by nuts and mix until well combined.
- Take a baking tray lined with butter paper and place the dough balls on the same with the help of a rounded spoon.
- Make sure that you keep some distance between two dough balls.
- Place in an oven preheated at 180°C or 355°F. Bake for 8–10 minutes.
- And your delicious chocolate chip cookies are ready. Let them cool and enjoy. You can even store them in an airtight container.

18

# Walnut and Fig Pie

There are times when you want to have a treat and you are not in a mood for cooking, you can prepare this delicious dessert much in advance and enjoy at such times.

## Method

- Refrigerate a pie crust placed in a pie tin for about half an hour until it sets.
- Chop the fig in quarters and place them in a large cooking pan.
- Add orange zest, granulated sugar, rum, water and vanilla extract.
- Cook this on medium flame until it starts boiling.
- Lower the flame and let it cook further for 10 minutes.
- Turn the flame off and let it cool at room temperature.
- Once cooled, place it in a food processor and grind until it becomes a rough paste. Add walnuts and grind to mix.
- Take the refrigerated crust out and place it on a baking tray lined with butter paper.
- Transfer the fudge mixture in the tin and level the surface.
- Bake for 20–25 minutes at 180°C or 355°F. You can also store this in a refrigerator up to two weeks.
- Serve it with vanilla ice cream.

## Ingredients

2 cups walnut, chopped
250 gm figs
200 ml water
100 ml rum
50 gm granulated sugar
½ tsp orange zest
½ tsp vanilla extract
1 pie crust

## Ingredients

- 250 gm butter
- 200 gm dark chocolate, break into small pieces
- 75 gm dried cherries
- 50 gm chopped nuts
- 80 gm cocoa powder, sifted
- 30 gm flour, sifted
- 1 tsp baking powder
- 360 gm demerara sugar
- 4 large eggs
- ½ tsp orange zest
- 250 ml fresh cream

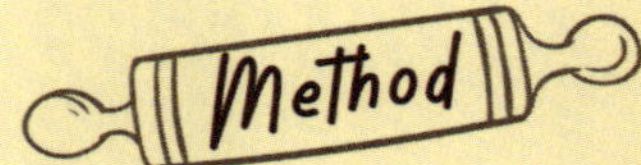


- Preheat the oven to 180°C or 355°F. Line a 25 cm square baking tin with butter paper.
- In a large bowl over some simmering water, melt the butter and the chocolate and mix until smooth. Add the cherries and nuts, if you are using them, and stir together.
- In a separate bowl, mix the cocoa powder, flour, baking powder and sugar, then add this to the chocolate, cherry and nut mixture. Stir them well. Beat the eggs and mix it until you have a silky consistency. Add the orange zest and fold it in the batter.
- Pour the brownie mix into the baking tray, and place in the oven for around 25 minutes. You don't want to overcook them; so unlike cakes, you don't want a skewer to come out all clean.

20

# Cinnamon and Oats Tea Cake

## Ingredients

- 1½ cups oats flour, sifted
- ½ cup milk
- ½ cup sugar
- ⅓ cup butter, at room temperature
- 1 egg
- 1 tsp pure vanilla extract
- ¼ tsp of cinnamon powder

There are always those times when you crave for a little something that you can serve up with drinks on the days you call your friends over. Cinnamon and Oats Tea Cake is the perfect gateway to keep your friends entranced with your preparations!

## Method

- In a bowl, take butter, sugar, vanilla and beat until the mixture turns whitish. Add egg and beat until well combined. Gradually add flour and milk. Add cinnamon powder, fold and mix the batter. Grease a cake tin with butter and put butter paper in the same.
- Now transfer the mixture into the tin and level it. Bake for 30–35 minutes in an oven preheated at 180°C or 355°F. Leave the cake for 10 minutes after removing from the oven. Then take it out on a wire rack. Brush melted butter on the cake while it is warm and sprinkle butter-sugar-vanilla mixture.

21

# Coconut Macaroons

This is a twist to the classic macaroons. The French recipe swings into the creamy goodness as we introduce coconuts to the recipe. The sweetness doubles up when coconuts come into the equation.

## Ingredients

4 egg whites
3 cups coconut (shredded)
½ cup sugar (granulated)

## Method

- Take the egg whites in a bowl, and whisk until frothy.
- Add sugar, mix it well, then add coconut and combine everything with the help of a spoon.
- Transfer the mixture into a piping bag, then line two pans with parchment paper and pipe small portions of the mixture on the paper.
- Bake for 15–20 minutes or until it is brown on the top in an oven preheated at 180°C or 355°F. Cool them before serving.

# Indian Delicacies

A pronounced yet discerning sweet tooth is what started my love for baking but while cakes and cookies find a firm place in my heart, *Phir bhi dil hai Hindustani!* So, my sweetest soft spot is reserved for Indian desserts.

Who can resist the creamy luxury of a lovingly made Seviyan Kheer? Or the crunch and crackle as you bite into a crisply golden Peanut Chikki? Would Diwali feel complete without your share of Kaju Katlis? Oh, the joy of digging into hot Jalebis and the dark tempting Gulab Jamuns at a wedding! As Indians, so much of our emotions and memories are wrapped up in our taste buds and love found in every bite of our desi desserts.

Be it our festivals or the glistening-with-ghee Moong Dal Halwa that your grandmother used to lovingly serve, there is so much history and warmth behind each of these delicacies. And that is what I hope to have replicated in bringing you my version of these classic Indian dessert recipes.

My own journey of cooking began when friends and family started appreciating the special Indian desserts that I would make and send over for them, during festivals like Diwali or on birthdays.

India as a country is so beautifully diverse – be it in language or cuisine, each state celebrates its own specialities. Yet there is also unity in diversity. Payasam for instance is made in so many ways in the different regions of India—some with rice, some with vermicelli, some rich in dry fruits and nuts, others subtly fragrant with the spices used. Yet all these different types of Payasam are considered auspicious and are traditionally served on birthdays or after a puja.

I feel blessed to be an Indian and to have been exposed to all these different kinds of desserts from different parts of my country and that is what I have tried to share with you in this section. Humble vegetables like Lauki (bottle gourd) can be turned into such delicious Indian desserts! So, from recipes for the softest Puran Polis to the creamiest Shrikhand and for the unexpectedly healthy desserts like Papaya Halwa to the steamed succulence of the perfect Modak, I hope you will try your hand at making these desi delights and get a delightful taste of India and its glorious heritage.

One of the most beloved desserts in the north Indian cuisines, Gulab Jamun is almost a universal favourite among people of all ages. You can devour it hot; you can pour scoops of ice cream to it for a cooling dish, you can stuff it with goodies like kesar and pista – there is really no end to the ways that you can enjoy this dish. Here is my recipe of perfecting the art of making these round pieces of deliciousness! This recipe makes twelve Gulab Jamuns.

## Ingredients

- 500 gm jaggery (soaked in 500 ml water)
- 300 gm fresh mawa
- 100 gm paneer (cottage cheese)
- 70 gm plain flour
- Pinch of baking powder
- ½ tsp green cardamom
- 7 to 8 cashews, finely chopped
- 7 to 8 almonds, finely chopped
- Ghee, for frying gulab jamuns

## Method

- To prepare the syrup for gulab jamun, heat a vessel and put jaggery and water, on a low flame until it dissolves! Let the jaggery dissolve completely into the water.
- In a bowl, take mawa and mash it well. Transfer it into a plate. In the same bowl, take paneer and crumble it to make a smooth dough, now put the mashed mawa in it followed by flour. Mix everything well and knead a soft dough out of it. Make sure the dough is smooth and has no lumps or cracks.
- Keep a frying pan on medium flame and add ghee in the pan for frying. To make the stuffing, take almonds, cashews, cardamom powder and a little mawa in a bowl and mix everything well. To prepare the gulab jamun flatten the dough ball with your fingers and top it up with some stuffing and close really well. Roll it out smoothly. You can also prepare gulab jamuns without stuffing.
- Once prepared, drop them into hot ghee and fry until golden brown. Strain the excess ghee as you take it out. Drop these fried gulab jamuns directly to the jaggery syrup, the syrup must be slightly warm. Press them down using a spoon to let the balls dip and soak it well in the syrup. Within 3–4 hours, gulab jamuns absorb the syrup well and turn sweet. Enjoy!

23

# Seviyan Kheer

Ever since I learned how to cook, Seviyan Kheer has been my go-to dish for the days I am feeling low. Not only is it super easy to make, but it brings back delicious memories of sitting with my family after dinner and being served Seviyan as the last dish. Because it is so easy to make and only requires ingredients that are easily available at home, anyone with a basic kitchen can attempt this lip-smacking dessert!

## Ingredients

- 2 tbsp ghee
- 750 ml milk
- 100 gm roasted vermicelli
- 75 gm brown sugar
- 20 gm cashew nuts (cut each cashew into 8 pieces)
- 4–5 almonds (cut them lengthwise into thin pieces)
- 4–5 small cardamoms
- 25 raisins

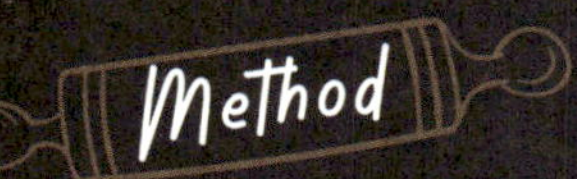


- Take some ghee in a heated pan, put vermicelli into the same and cook it on a low flame. Keep stirring it continuously until it turns golden brown. Now, transfer the vermicelli in a plate.
- In a thick frying pan, add milk to boil. Once the milk starts boiling add vermicelli. Keep stirring continuously and cook until the milk starts boiling again.
- When the milk starts reducing, add cashews, raisins and sugar and lower the flame. Cook for 5–7 minutes more.
- Turn the flame off when the vermicelli softens. At this stage, add cardamom granules. Garnish with chopped almonds. Serve it hot or chilled.

# 24 Lauki Halwa

Lauki Halwa deserves a special mention in this book. Lauki (bottle gourd) is classically known to be a boring vegetable. Let me tell you that it is a misconception. There are various ways in which you can make it super interesting and lauki halwa is one of the ways. Take it from someone who refused to eat lauki as a kid, lauki halwa is one of the most delicious preparations that can be made.

## Ingredients

- 1 tbsp ghee
- 2 cups tightly packed grated bottle gourd
- 2 cups full-fat milk, chilled after boiling
- 7–8 tbsp jaggery or coconut sugar
- 5–6 green cardamoms, powdered
- 3–4 tbsp chopped nuts
- 1 tbsp raisins, soaked
- 5–6 sliced almonds for garnish

## Method

- In a heavy pan or kadhai heat ghee on a medium flame. Now put grated bottle gourd and saute it. Stir often and saute until the moisture dries off. Then add the full-fat milk.
- Mix everything well and cook until it boils. Keep cooking until three-fourths of the milk is reduced and absorbed. Add jaggery and chopped nuts. Mix well and cook until the mixture starts releasing ghee.
- Turn the flame off. Add raisins and mix well. Garnish with dry fruits and serve.

# Moong Dal Halwa

Moong dal halwa is a great favourite among the elders. My father doesn't have a sweet tooth, but one thing he never fails to miss is moong dal halwa. Every birthday, we make sure to create the most delicious, the purest form of Moong Dal Halwa that he can devour and relish with those he loves. So here I am, sharing the recipe with you!

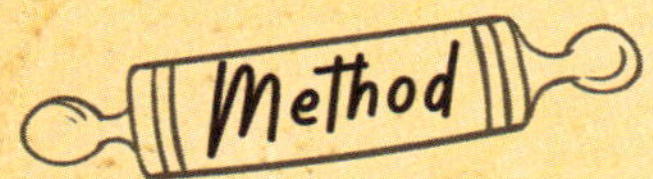

## Method

- Grind the soaked moong dal. Do not grind it perfectly fine. In a heated pan, put ghee followed by ground moong dal. Cook it for 15–20 minutes while stirring it continuously on medium flame. Transfer it into a plate. In the same frying pan, take some mawa, cook it on a low flame, then add moong dal into the same.
- On the other hand, take some water in a utensil and heat it, then add equal amount of sugar. Let it cook for 5–7 minutes after the sugar melts. Then add this syrup in the moong dal along with cashew nuts and raisins. Stir it on a low flame for about 5–7 minutes.
- Take out the halwa in a bowl and garnish it with almonds. Serve it hot!

## Ingredients

150 gm jaggery
100 gm moong dal (soaked for 4–5 hrs)
100 gm ghee
50 gm mawa
20 dried raisins, soaked
20 cashew nuts (cut each cashew into four pieces)
5 almonds (cut them lengthwise into thin slices)
Cardamom powder

26

# Puran Poli

This is one of the most famous Maharashtrian desserts. In fact, I will go ahead and call it a full meal by itself. To me, Puran Poli is the most delicious and wholesome part of the Maharashtrian culture. Pour a generous amount of ghee on to the puran poli and you have a heart-warming dish in front of you! The flavour is so rich and self-indulgent, you will be craving for more even though there is no place left in your tummy! This recipe makes 6 of them.

## Ingredients

400 gm wheat flour
150 gm split Bengal gram, soaked for 4–5 hrs
50 gm jaggery
8–10 green cardamom
1 tbsp ghee
Salt to taste

## Method

- Sift flour, add ghee and salt. Mix it well and knead a soft dough using warm water. Cover and let it rest for about 20 minutes. Boil the soaked gram in a pressure cooker with 2–3 tbsp. water. Turn the flame off after a whistle. Let it cool and then grind it in a mixer without water. Make sure to grind it fine.
- In a vessel, take one tablespoon ghee. Heat it well. Put small pieces of jaggery in the hot ghee and melt it. After that add the lentil into the same. Cook it for five minutes. Turn the flame off and add powdered green cardamom. The puran is ready.
- Heat a griddle. Make a small ball of dough, flatten and stuff two tablespoon of puran. Seal and press between your palms. Rub this stuffed ball with flour and roll into a round 6–7-inches in diameter with a rolling pin.
- Put puran poli on the griddle. Apply ghee on both sides and fry till it turns brown, turning regularly. Make all the remaining puran poli similarly. You can serve it hot with warm milk.

Having lived in Maharashtra for more than ten years now, its culture has had a considerable impact on me. Every year, I cannot help but join the throngs of devotees on Ganesh Chaturthi. One of the most surprising sweets I came across was modak. Made of rice flour, modak is chewy on the outside and has a sweet, crumbly deliciousness on the inside.

## Ingredients

- 1 cup coconut, grated
- 1 cup jaggery
- 1 cup water
- 1 cup rice flour
- 2 tsp ghee
- A pinch of nutmeg
- A pinch of saffron
- A pinch of salt

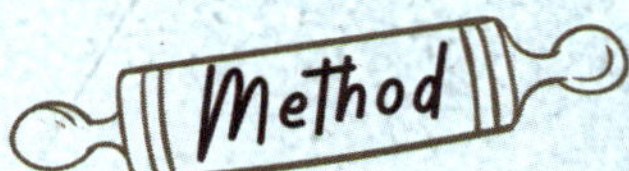


- In a heated pan, add grated coconut and jaggery. Stir it for 5 minutes and then add nutmeg and saffron. Mix well.
- In a deep pan boil water with some ghee, add salt and flour. Mix well. Cover the dish and cook till it is half done.
- Grease a bowl with some ghee. Take out the dough in the bowl and knead it well while it is hot. Now take a little dough, roll it into a ball, flatten it well, shape the edges into a flower pattern. Put a spoonful of the filling on to the dough and seal it.
- Put the dumplings in a muslin cloth and steam them for 10–15 minutes. Serve.

28

# Peanut Chikki

Apart from masala chai and sunny mornings, the best thing about winters is the Peanut Chikki. Crunchy and sweet, chikki is truly the embodiment of an Indian version of high protein bars. With jaggery being healthy for the heart and body in general and peanuts being a rich protein source, you can enjoy a chikki without any remorse!

## Ingredients

1 cup roasted peanuts
1 cup jaggery crumbled
2 tbsp ghee

- In a heated pan, take crumbled jaggery. Add some ghee into the same. Stir continuously and melt it. Keep the flame low. Cook it for 1–2 more minutes after it melts. The syrup must be of uniform consistency. Keeping the flame low add peanuts in the syrup. Mix well and turn the flame off.
- Now, grease a board and spatula you are going to use with ghee. Pour the mixture on the board and spread with the help of a spatula. Use a rolling pin if needed, but do not forget to grease the same.
- Mark the chikki when the mixture is slightly cool and separate it from the board once cooled completely. The deliciously healthy and crunchy peanut chikki is ready.

# 29 Kaju Katli

Every Diwali, you get a boxful of the same old boring kaju katli, right? But I have to set the record straight; to me, Kaju Katli is like the vanilla of sweets. Available everywhere but it's only the right preparation that can blow your mind. Here is how you can make your own batch of some lip-smacking katli!

## Ingredients

500 gm cashew nuts (soaked in warm water for 1 hour)
500 gm powdered sugar
1 tsp ground cardamom
2 tbsp pure ghee

## Method

- Remove the cashews from water and grind the soaked cashews finely. In this paste add the powdered sugar.
- Transfer this mixture in a heated pan and cook this mixture on low flame. After a while the mixture will become thick, at this stage turn off the flame and add ground cardamom in it. Let the paste cool for 10–15 minutes.
- Once this mixture cools off, transfer it into a well-greased tray and cut it in desired shapes. Fresh kaju katli is ready to be served. You can store this upto ten days.

30

# Fruit Jalebi

I might have been a little partial to the chikki earlier. Waking up early in the cold Sunday mornings of Shimla, I remember my father going to a milk shop taking me and my sibling tottering along with him. Oh, the sweet taste of crispy hot golden jalebis! My mouth waters even as I write about it. You know what adds even more flavour to it? Dipping them in plain hot milk! The flavour is simply out of the world and it is something you should definitely give a try.

## Ingredients

- 400 gm jaggery
- 1½ cups plain flour
- ½ spoon yeast
- 1 tbsp milk
- 1 tsp lemon juice
- ¼ tsp saffron
- ¼ tsp cardamom
- Ghee, for frying
- ½ cup assorted fruits

## Method

- Soak the yeast granules in warm water for 10–12 minutes then strain it. In a bowl, take plain flour, add the yeast water, also add normal water and make a flowing medium-consistency batter. Leave this liquid mixture for 10–12 hours for fermentation.
- In a pot, add sugar and pour equal amount of water. Boil the syrup until it reaches one string consistency. Add lemon juice followed by saffron and cardamom. Stir the fermented flour adequately and transfer it into a squeezable sauce bottle.
- In a pan, heat ghee for frying. The pan should be bigger with lesser height. The ghee should be heated enough on medium-high flame. At this stage, put small portion of the batter into ghee, if it comes up immediately without browning then the ghee is heated enough. Start making jalebi. After they turn pinkish, take out the fried jalebis and submerge them in the sweet syrup.
- After 5 minutes, take the jalebis out from the syrup and put them in a plate along with the fruits. Your jalebi is ready to be served.

31

# Payasam

*Payasam* is the south Indian version of kheer. It is creamy, and with the first bite into the payasam, I bet a floodgate of happiness will open up for you!

## Ingredients

2 cups water
½ cup medium grain basmati rice
1½ cup jaggery
3 tbsp raisins
2½ tbsp ghee
1 tbsp cashews

## Method

- In a vessel, take some rice and boil it on high flame. Keep stirring continuously to avoid sticking or burning.
- When the rice is cooked, add jaggery and ghee. Keep stirring and cook until it thickens. Garnish with raisins and cashews and add some more ghee. Serve.

# Rabri Malpua

Personally, I believe that rabri malpua is the true representation of Indian desserts. It is dripping in sweetness, has the mind-numbing creamy taste of milk, and is full of goodies like saffron, pistachios, almonds and cardamom. With the perfect rabri malpua, you can win people's hearts. All you have to do is achieve that insane flavour.

## Ingredients

**For Rabri:**
1 litre milk
1 cup sugar
½ tsp saffron
1 tsp pistachios
1 tsp almonds
1 tsp cardamom powder

**For Syrup:**
2 cups sugar
2 cups water
A few saffron strands
1 tsp cardamom powder
2 tsp almonds

**For Malpua:**
1 cup plain flour
¼ cup sooji (semolina)
½ cup khoya
2 tsp sugar (powdered)
1 tsp fennel seeds
1 cup water, 2 cups ghee
Blueberries for garnishing

## Method

- In a pan, boil milk. Add sugar, saffron, pistachios, almond and cardamom powder. Keep the rabri aside. Mix thoroughly to make a smooth batter.
- To prepare syrup, take some water and sugar in a pan. Bring it to boil. Add some saffron and cardamom powder into the same.
- In a bowl, take plain flour, semolina, khoya, powdered sugar, fennel seeds and water. Whisk well.
- Now, on a flat pan add ghee, a spoonful of the batter and cook until golden. Then transfer it into the syrup. Soak well, take out. Put some rabri on top of it, add blueberries and serve.

# 33 Mango Shrikhand

Shrikhand is one of the most delicious and the most beneficial desserts you can possibly have. Full of probiotics, a good and chilled shrikhand will not only do great things to your body but also nourish your soul! And when you add mango to this already seductive recipe, Mango Shrikhand becomes a dish to die for!

## Ingredients

3 cups yogurt
1 cup mango puree
⅓ cup honey
¼ tsp crushed cardamom

**For Garnishing**

¼ cup mango, cut into small pieces
1 tbsp sliced pistachios, almonds for garnish

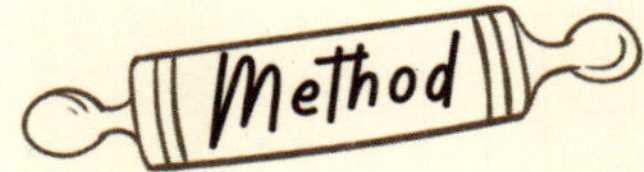

## Method

- Take a strainer, keep a muslin cloth on top of the same. Pour the yogurt on it and strain well. Collect the excess water in a bowl. Gently squeeze to take out the excess water. Move it into a refrigerator.
- Take it out after 4 hours. It will become thick like a cheese ball. Add mango pulp, honey and cardamom powder to the yogurt.
- Mix well until it's uniformly smooth. Garnish with mango pieces, almonds and pistachios. Serve chilled.

# Sitaphal Rabri

Oh, to eat a desi, classic rabri! Some of my favourite childhood memories are going to the halwai's shop and eating rabri out of a dona (bowl made out of dried leaves). The rustic flavour is unmatchable! I am presenting the same here with a twist of sitaphal (custard apple). I am sure you will love this delicious recipe.

## Ingredients

- 1 cup milk
- 1 tbsp condensed milk
- 1 tsp cardamom powder
- 2 custard apple's pulp
- ½ cup mixed dry fruits

## Method

- Take a pan, pour milk and boil it. Then add condensed milk and keep stirring till it thickens.
- Add the pulp of custard apple and cardamom powder, and mix it well. Garnish it with dry fruits. Serve.

35

# Papaya Halwa

Papayas are unique fruits. Known for their medicinal properties and distinct flavour, they are a favourite of many. It is a fruit that keeps your digestive tract well functioning and your skin glowing. But what about those who simply detest papaya? There are definitely no in-between opinions about papayas. Papaya Halwa doesn't discriminate. Meant to be loved by everyone, even those who are not as fond of the fruit, papaya halwa is full of goodness.

## Ingredients

- 1 medium semi-ripe papaya, grated
- 4–5 tbsp jaggery/coconut sugar
- 2–3 tbsp ghee
- 2 tbsp almond powder
- ½ tsp green cardamom powder
- 12–15 halved cashews
- 4–5 sliced almonds for garnish

## Method

- Take a thick pan or kadhai and heat ghee. Put papaya in it and cook for 15 minutes. Stir often.
- The fruit will release juice, change colour, and become translucent. Add jaggery and keep cooking for about 20 minutes more. Keep stirring. At this stage the mixture will start releasing the ghee. Add almond and stir.
- Cook for 5 minutes and then add cashews. Cook for about a minute and turn the flame off. Serve hot.

# Quickie Desserts

If there is one thing that is at a premium in our modern world, it is time. Everyone is running at breakneck speed all the time and for people who have to cook regularly and have a million other responsibilities to take care of as well, quick easy recipes are the biggest blessings!

This becomes even more true when it comes to making desserts. After all, it is so much easier to just order in some ice cream in summer or some gajar ka halwa during winter. But outside desserts are not always the healthiest alternatives, not to mention that they can quickly burn a hole in your wallet because – let us face it – high quality desserts can be quite expensive.

So, what if I told you that you could whip up your own delicious desserts at home without investing too much time or effort into making them? This is where everyday appliances like your microwave and the most basic ingredients like bananas and plain bread become your best friends!

Just try your hand at whipping up my Dry Fruit Laddoos or my divinely delicious Peanut Butter Cups – all made with the simplest ingredients found easily in every regular household. Then there is a yummy Mocha Truffles and my Microwave Banana Pudding and Microwave Eggless Brownie recipes that are instant crowd pleasers, that look elaborate and taste heavenly but take only minutes to make!

Don't blame me if once you try your hand at making these quickie desserts, you just can't stop – or rather if your family members keep asking for more! These desserts are really simple, time-saving, deceptively delicious and very addictive!

36

# Peanut Butter Cups

Made especially for those who have a major sweet tooth but do not have the time to create dishes that will satiate their cravings every day. Sharing with you this recipe with my secret ingredient poha (flattened rice). These Peanut Butter Cups are meant to be made in one batch that you can reach out for whenever you crave a delicious sweet bite!

## Ingredients

1 cup chocolate, melted

½ cup creamy peanut butter

3 tbsp poha, flattened rice, sifted

## Method

- Prepare a cupcake tin with six liners. In a bowl, take peanut butter, poha and powdered sugar and beat until smooth.
- Spread melted chocolate in the liners. Now put a spoonful of peanut butter batter on top of the same. Cover with some more chocolate and smoothen the top.
- Refrigerate for an hour until the chocolate sets. Then remove it from the liners.

# 37 1 Minute Microwave Eggless Brownie

You know those midnight sweet urges that are hard to ignore? This is a recipe that can easily satisfy that sweet tooth of yours. All it takes is a few ingredients, a microwave, and the dedication to appease your tummy!

## Ingredients

½ cup milk
3 tbsp olive oil
3 tbsp oats flour
3 tbsp cocoa powder
2 tbsp brown sugar
½ tsp vanilla essence
1 pinch salt

## Method

- In a microwave-friendly mug take sugar, milk and vanilla essence and mix until the sugar dissolves. Now add oil, flour, cocoa powder and salt. Mix till well combined.
- Now microwave for a minute (if your microwave is of 1200 W, microwave for 1.5–2 minutes). Take out and let it cool. Serve with whipped cream or top it with vanilla ice cream.

# Mocha Truffles

38

Truffles are the most indulgent treats that can ever exist. Its richness and smooth flavour are something to die for! Mocha Truffles dessert is for the days when you want to do something extra special for your partner. Rich and delicious, you can achieve this dessert in a matter of minutes!

## Ingredients

400 gm dark chocolate, melted

225 gm cream cheese, softened

35–40 gm oats, crushed

## Method

- In a bowl, take the crushed oats and cheese. Mix until well combined. Refrigerate the mixture for an hour. Take it out and roll them into ball size.
- Take a baking sheet and line it with parchment paper. Dip the rolled balls into melted dark chocolate and place on the baking sheet. Sprinkle the reserved cookies on the truffles.

39

# Peanut Butter Cupcakes

It is midnight, and you are really craving a cake but don't want to go through the trouble of spending another 30–40 minutes trying to bake a cake. What do you do? Create cupcakes! This short and sweet recipe is the perfect answer to your midnight cravings!

## Ingredients

- 3 eggs
- 1 cup white coconut sugar
- ⅔ cup creamy peanut butter
- 1½ cups coconut flour
- ⅓ cup olive oil
- 1 tbsp vanilla essence
- ½ cup milk
- 1tsp baking powder
- ½ tsp baking soda

## Method

- Heat oven at 180°C or 355°F for 10 minutes. Combine all the ingredients in a bowl and make a smooth batter.
- Transfer the batter in greased cupcake moulds lined with cupcake liners leaving 1inch on the top.
- Bake until a toothpick pierced in the centre comes out clean and the cupcakes are light golden in colour.

40

# Mango Ice Cream

Mangoes are everyone's favourite. It does not matter if you're old or young, I can bet that every summer you look forward to devouring mangoes! This is an easy and very accessible recipe that anyone can make, even if you are a ten-year-old!

## Method

- Take a large ripe mango, peel it and chop. Make a purée of the same with the help of a food processor.
- Now add milk and banana. Mix it once again with the help of the food processor. Spoon into a box and freeze. Garnish with nuts before serving!

## Ingredients

1 banana
1 large ripe mango
6 tbsp almond milk
1–2 drops mango essence

# Dry Fruit Laddoos

Any kind of laddoos is my personal favourite. Dry Fruit Laddoos are perfect if you are looking for a healthy snack full of nutrient. I make it during the Diwali time when there is a slight chill in the air and one can enjoy it the most!

## Ingredients

40 gm figs
30 gm chopped cashew
30 gm chopped pistachio
20 gm chopped almond
20 gm mixed seeds
80 gm dates

## Method

- In a large bowl, add chopped roasted almonds, roasted cashews, roasted pistachios and mixed seeds. Mix well.
- After a few minutes add mashed dates and figs and blend them. Let it cool and then make medium equal-sized balls. Serve and enjoy.

42

# Crepes

When I think of all preparations, dessert crepes are the most fun – the lightest, and the most delicious preparations that can be made. You can add your own preference of fruits to these to make them even more fun! Add a mango, strawberries, drizzle a lot of chocolate, dollop of cream! You name it! Any addition of your choice is a great addition to these dessert crepes!

## Ingredients

1 egg
1½ cups milk
1¼ cups coconut flour
2 tsp olive oil/butter
½ tsp pure lemon extract
Lemon juice
Maple syrup for sprinkling
½ cup assorted fruits

## Method

- Whisk egg and milk in a bowl. In another bowl, add flour and transfer the egg and milk mixture into the same. Add the lemon extract and whisk well. Cover it and set aside for about 30 minutes.
- Put a non-stick frying pan over medium heat and add oil or butter and spread it uniformly.
- Pour a spoonful of batter and spread evenly to make a thin layer.
- Let it cook until light golden, then flip and cook for a minute more.
- Transfer the same to a plate.
- Fold the crepes in quarters.
- Use a bit of lemon juice and maple syrup for drizzling.
- Serve with assorted fruits!

43

# Healthy Bite on the Go!

This recipe is one of my favourites! I prepare it beforehand and when I am in a rush to leave home, I just grab a few to eat on the way! Healthy, filling and delicious! If you are a sweet lover like me, try this out!

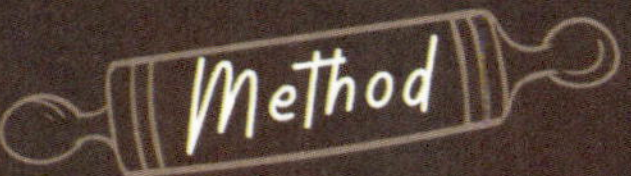

## Method

- Take a large pan, add crushed biscuits, cocoa, almonds, walnuts, raisins. Prepare a tin by greasing with butter and lining a parchment paper. Transfer the mixture into the prepared tin. Microwave for 5 secs.
- Microwave both the chocolates until melted. Transfer the melted chocolate over the mixture in the tin. Coat it in chocolate completely with the help of a spoon. Refrigerate for 2 hours until it sets. You can also leave it overnight to set.

## Ingredients

Oats biscuits, crushed
100 gm milk chocolate
100 gm dark chocolate
6 tsp cocoa powder
Handful of almonds, walnuts and raisins

# Banoffee Split

Who hasn't heard about Banana split? This is my take on the same dish – combining two of my favourite sweet foods, chocolate, and bananas. Banoffee Split is a fool proof recipe. Give it a try!

## Ingredients

2 small ripe bananas
4 scoops ice cream
1 chocolate bar, chopped into small chunks
Caramel sauce
Butter

## Method

- Take a saucepan, put chocolate bar, cream, butter and cook well until it becomes a smooth sauce.
- Take a serving plate and keep the banana divided in two parts on the plate. Add the warm sauce. Serve.

**Note**

You can make the sauce by adding water, sugar and butter in a pan and let the sugar melt and caramelize, once done, add cream and whisk quickly until the desired consistency!

45

# Coconut Laddoos

With the arrival of festivals, come desserts! As for myself, I don't really wait for festivals, I just love sweets! We have a never-ending number of traditional desserts. This is also one of those desserts, which I used to love as a child, and even as an adult I love it. I am sure you will love this quick, simple and extremely delicious recipe.

## Ingredients

1 cup desiccated coconut

½ cup khoya

2 tbsp jaggery powder

A pinch of cardamom powder

## Method

- Take a heated pan, add desiccated coconut and roast it well. Then add khoya, cardamom powder and powdered jaggery. Keep stirring. Transfer in a bowl when well combined. Let it cool at room temperature.
- Brush your hands with powdered sugar and make laddoos. Roll in desiccated coconut and serve.

# Microwave Banana Pudding

A recipe made for those who love a ripe banana! You know how sometimes; you buy too many bananas and do not know what to do with it? Fret not, this recipe will help you gobble them up so quickly, you will wonder where they disappeared!

## Ingredients

100 gm butter, softened
100 gm coconut sugar
100 gm oats flour
2 ripe bananas
2 eggs
2 tsp cinnamon powder
2 tbsp milk
Choco chips (a handful)
Icing sugar, toffee sauce and ice cream

## Method

- Take a 1 litre-sized baking tray. Put the butter into the same and microwave for a minute. Take the tray out, add mashed banana, sugar, flour, cinnamon, eggs and milk. Mix until well combined.
- Slice the remaining banana on top and add choco chips. Microwave for 8 minutes. Take it out. Enjoy!

# Indian Fusion Desserts

India is one of the most multi-dimensional, diverse and vibrant countries in the world. It is also very embracing of other cultures, cuisines and people. While every part of our country, every state has a unique cuisine to call its own, with time there has also been a lot of intermingling and coming together of different flavours, ingredients and techniques. And that is the best thing about fusion food! When done right, fusion food brings together the very best of two entirely separate cuisines and worlds.

Fusion food has been my special area of interest and featured prominently during my stint in MasterChef India (Season 2), which I won, back in 2011. The curiosity and excitement of bringing together unexpected flavours and ingredients was always there and has steadily grown in me since then. And that spills over into what lies closest to my heart – Indian Fusion Desserts. Which is also why this section is the longest in this book with the maximum number of recipes! It's as if once I start creating and experimenting with fusion desserts, I just cannot stop!

Don't worry, none of these recipes are overly complicated and don't require exotic or hard-to-find ingredients. They do, however, marry two very distinct flavour profiles in ways that may surprise and delight you! Some quintessentially Indian yet distinctly international recipes in this section include Beetroot Halwa, Pineapple Sandesh, Baked Chilli Yogurt and Makhana Pudding, to name just a few. Years of my professional experience and tinkering around with ideas and ingredients and of course my heart and passion, have gone into creating these recipes and all of them are tried and tested and have met with resounding appreciation from family, friends, customers (at my restaurants) and other professional chefs – both in India and abroad.

I hope you will jump right into trying out my various Indian Fusion Dessert recipes. Keep an open mind, heart and palate, play around with combos and ingredients you may have never thought of putting together before, and I guarantee that a whole new world of delicious flavours will open up to delight you and your loved ones!

47

# Makhana Pudding

Makhana is a curious ingredient. You can roast them, fry them, season them, turn them into a sabzi, each preparation will give makhanas a different texture. Because they are so rich in protein and loved by people of all age groups, I decided to incorporate them into desserts to create a dish that is not only rich in protein but also delicious to the tongue!

## Ingredients

4 cups whole milk
1½ cups makhana (puffed lotus seeds)
½ cup rice, cooked and mashed
½ cup raw honey
2 tbsp almonds, blanched and sliced
2 tbsp pistachios, blanched and sliced
2 tsp ghee
¼ tsp cardamom, crushed
Few strands of saffron

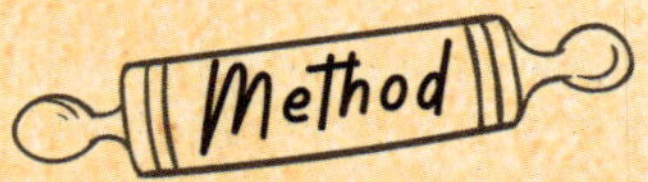


## Method

- To make the makhanas crisp, microwave them for half a minute. In a pan, add makhana followed by almonds and cook.
- After 2 minutes add milk, mashed rice. Keeping the flame on medium high boil the milk. Lower the flame once the milk starts boiling. Cook for another 18–20 minutes. Add some cardamom, saffron and pistachios.
- Now take a thick-bottomed pan, grease it and let it heat. Once heated, add sugar. Keep stirring until the sugar melts and changes the colour to brown.
- Pour the syrup over the prepared mixture and your Makhana Pudding is ready.

48

# Rava Cake

It is the most unexpected and the most pleasantly surprising textures in this recipe. A rava cake is just as fluffy, just as mind-numbingly delicious and the best part is that it is healthier because it's made of semolina. If you want to impress your guests, I think a Rava Cake would be the perfect way to do so.

## Ingredients

1 cup plain flour
½ cup rava (semolina)
1 cup milk, adjust consistency
¼ cup curd, whisked
2 tbsp tutti frutti
¼ tsp cardamom powder
¾ tsp baking powder
½ tsp baking soda
Handful of dry fruits, chopped
A pinch of salt

**For the syrup**

1 cup jaggery
A few strands of saffron

## Method

- In a bowl, add rava, plain flour, salt, cardamom powder, curd, milk and mix everything well. Soak for about half an hour.
- After that add baking soda and baking powder into the mixture. Add tutti frutti, then whisk and transfer into a cake tin. Bake at 180°C or 355°F for 40 minutes. Then take it out and let it cool.
- Meanwhile, make a sweet syrup with jaggery and water and let it boil until jaggery is fully dissolved, add a few strands of saffron. Let it cool and pour over the cake. It will soak the syrup and become really refreshing in taste.

# Pineapple Sandesh

I have never met anyone who doesn't like a chilled sandesh. And I know no one who has anything against pineapples. Just how pineapples taste fresh and light, sandesh is a Bengali dish that is fluffy and light and refreshes you with every bite. For me, it only made sense to experiment and see if we could combine the two elements together. Voila! A delightfully fresh preparation for all of you to enjoy!

## Ingredients

4 cups whole milk
3 tbsp lemon juice
3 tbsp jaggery
2 tbsp sliced pistachios
¼ tsp cardamom
6 slices of pineapple, canned

## Method

- In a pan, heat milk on high flame till it boils. Keep stirring. When the milk comes to boil, add lemon juice and keep stirring. Stir gently. Now you will see that the milk starts separating and paneer is formed. Once it has separated completely, drain the whey with the help of a muslin cloth. Then rinse it in cold water and squeeze.
- Once it is well drained, knead a smooth dough of the paneer. Now add jaggery and cardamom powder, keep kneading until the jaggery mixes. Spread the pineapple slices on a dry surface and pat the muslin cloth on the same.
- Now spread the prepared paneer, also called sandesh. Put pineapple on top of it and garnish with sliced pistachios. Cut in desired shapes and refrigerate it for about an hour and serve.

# 50 Custard Bites

I love high teas, and this one is a perfect dessert to be shared with tea. Quick, easy and praiseworthy!

## Method

- Take milk, honey, cream, corn starch, cardamom powder and saffron in a bowl. Mix well and make sure there are no lumps in the mixture.
- Keep the flame medium and boil while stirring continuously. Lower the flame and keep stirring till the mixture thickens. Once it thickens, turn the flame off and add dry fruits.
- The custard is ready. Spread it on the bread slices and toast them. Sprinkle toasted coconut and serve.

## Ingredients

12 thin slices of Italian bread bruschetta
1¼ cups milk
¼ cup thick coconut cream
¼ cup honey
2 tbsp melted butter
1½ tbsp corn starch
2 tbsp toasted coconut shreds
A few strands of saffron
A pinch of cardamom powder

# 51 Pineapple Sheera

I have said it before; I'll say it again; pineapple brings in the tropical vibes which I love! It is so refreshing and reminds me of summer. This is my take on the summery goodness: to make it palatable to even those who do not relish pineapples.

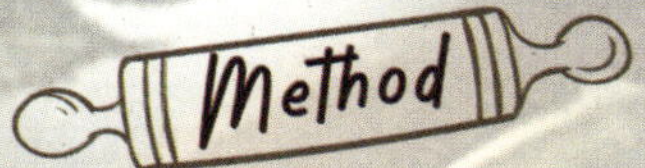

## Method

- In a heated pan, take some ghee and put semolina and roast until golden brown. Make sure you stir it continuously. Once well roasted take it out in a plate. Add pineapple paste into the same pan and cook until it turns light brown. Now add roasted semolina.
- Keep the flame low and cook until the semolina puffs up. Then add sugar and cook until sugar mixes well. Add chopped dry fruits, followed by cardamom powder. Cook until it becomes thick in consistency.
- At the final stage add some ghee into the same. Garnish with dry fruits and serve warm.

## Ingredients

100 gm pineapple (ground into paste)
100 gm rava (semolina)
1 tbsp ghee
10–12 almonds
10–12 cashew nuts
½ cup sugar
4–5 green cardamoms, powdered
8–10 pistachios, finely chopped

52

# Beetroot Halwa

More often than not, beetroot is something not many people like eating. In Sindhi culture however, Beetroot Halwa is very prevalent. Not only does it hold an earthy flavour of beet but also provides its goodness.

## Ingredients

- 4 cups grated beetroot
- 2 tbsp ghee
- 2 tbsp sugar
- 1 tsp cardamom powder
- 2 tbsp finely chopped cashew nuts (fried or roasted)
- ½ cup full-fat milk

## Method

- Take a non-stick pan, heat it and add ghee. Once it is heated, transfer the beetroot in the pan and cook it for 4–5 minutes.
- Keep stirring occasionally, then add sugar, milk and cardamom powder. Cover it and let it cook for about 10 minutes. Keep stirring in between.
- After 10 minutes, remove the lid and let the liquid evaporate. Stir continuously. Garnish with cashew nuts and serve warm.

# Baked Chilli Yogurt

Sharing with you one of my superhit winning recipe from MasterChef days. It won the heart of the judges and got me closer to the title.

## Ingredients

1 cup hung curd
2 Thai red chillies (finely chopped)
3 tbsp honey
1 tsp vanilla essence
1 egg
Assorted fresh fruits for serving!

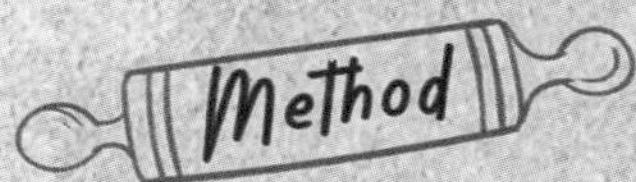

## Method

- In a bowl, mix everything until well combined.
- Grease ramekins with cooking oil lightly.
- Then add the batter to the ramekins.
- Bake in a preheated oven at 180°C or 355°F for 15 minutes.
- Take it out of the oven and then transfer on to a plate.
- Garnish with fresh fruits and serve.

# No-Bake Choco-Walnut Tarts

Here is an easy way of creating unique desserts that will steal the hearts of your guests. All you have to do is buy a packet of delicious Oreo cookies (we all know how beloved they are to all of us) and get into the kitchen!

## Ingredients

- 140 gm chopped dark cooking chocolate
- 40 ml coconut milk
- 20–25 crushed walnuts
- 3 tbsp Oreo cookies, powdered

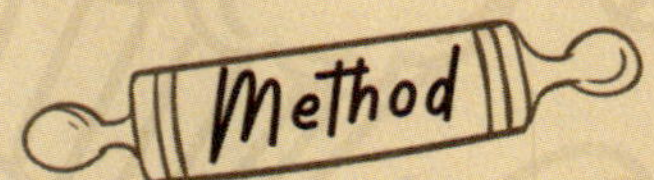

## Method

- Take crushed walnuts in a bowl and mix with Oreo cookies. Transfer the mixture into a small tart mould, 2 to 3 inches in size, and press it gently. Refrigerate for half an hour.
- Separately add chocolate into warm coconut milk, cover until the chocolate melts. Now take the refrigerated tarts out. Put the freshly made choco sauce on the same and refrigerate for 2–3 hours until set! Your choco-walnut tarts are ready!

# Chocolate Duo Mousse

Chocolate, as we all know, is the source of heavenly bliss. But what if I told you that you could double the heavenly bliss? Chocolate Duo Mousse is an easy recipe to achieve the dish, if you put your mind into it. All you have to do is hoard a ton of chocolates and create a dish that will have you comatose, counting the days when you can have the dish again!

## Ingredients

- 50 ml heavy cream
- 100 gm dark chocolate
- 50 ml whipped cream
- 10 ml brandy
- Fruit of your choice

## Method

- Cut dark chocolate into small pieces.
- Keep them aside separately.
- In a pan, take some cream and heat it.
- Pour the hot cream directly over the chopped chocolate.
- Let it melt. Set it aside to cool for a few minutes.
- Now add some whipped cream and brandy and whisk it well.
- Spoon out the Chocolate Duo Mousse in serving glasses. You can enjoy it simply or with a fruit of your choice. Refrigerate the mousse and serve it chilled!

56

# Strawberry Banana Coconut Pop

Bringing health into desserts is something that I have always aspired to do. With someone who has a sweet tooth, I find it difficult to choose between my cravings and health. This is why I have been exploring ways of satiating my cravings with healthy alternatives. Here is one such recipe!

## Ingredients

2 cups coconut milk
2 cups strawberry, raspberry, diced
1 banana, sliced
3 tbsp honey
1 tbsp lime juice
2 tbsp maple syrup

## Method

- In a large bowl, take banana, strawberry, raspberry. Mix well. Further add lime juice and maple syrup. In a bowl, take coconut milk, strawberries, banana, and honey. Blend both the mixtures until it turns into a smooth batter.
- Pour the mixture into Popsicle moulds and refrigerate until it sets. It may take four hours. Unmould the Popsicles and enjoy. Mix well, slide them in sticks and serve.

57

# Banana Berry Fruit

Personally, I am a big fan of fruit. The freshness from the goodness of bananas with various exotic berries is outstanding! Here is how you can truly bring out the flavours of these fruits!

## Ingredients

3 bananas, sliced
340 gm fresh strawberry, quartered
340 gm fresh raspberry
3 tbsp lime juice
1 tbsp maple syrup

## Method

- In a large bowl, take banana, strawberry, raspberry. Mix well. Further add lime juice and maple syrup.
- Mix well, slide them in sticks and serve.

58

# Mango Coconut Frozen Yogurt

One thing I always look forward to during summers is that the markets are flooded with mangoes! Everywhere you look there is that delicious fragrance of mangoes, undeniably alluring! Mango Coconut Frozen Yogurt is not only soothing to your soul in the blistering heat, but is also full of health benefits because of the probiotics in the yogurt.

## Ingredients

3 cups fresh mango
½ cup coconut milk
½ cup yogurt
2 tbsp honey

## Method

- Mix mango, coconut milk, yogurt and honey in a bowl and blend into a smooth mixture.
- Freeze for 2 hours and serve it with your favourite toppings.

59

# Chocolate Fudge

On days when you are feeling lazy, this recipe of easy chocolate fudge will be your saviour! You can whip up a mouth-watering Chocolate Fudge within 10 minutes with this recipe!

## Ingredients

500 gm milk chocolate
395 gm sweetened condensed milk
80 gm roasted pistachios, chopped
60 gm butter

## Method

- In a bowl, take butter, condensed milk and chocolate, microwave until melted. Add chopped nuts and stir.
- Prepare a pan by greasing with butter and transfer the mixture in the pan. Level the surface. Refrigerate until set. Cut into bite size and serve.

60

# Chocolate Coconut Balls

Easy to make, easier to devour! These Chocolate Coconut Balls are specially for those who love the coconut flavour. What sets these balls apart from the rest of the preparation is that you can reap the benefits as soon as you sow them! With no heat involved, you can ask your kids to participate in the same!

## Ingredients

- 4½ cups coconut flakes
- 2 tbsp condensed milk
- 150 gm melted semi-sweet chocolate
- 1 tsp vanilla extract

## Method

- Pulse the coconut flakes lightly and add condensed milk followed by vanilla extract. Mix well and refrigerate the mixture for about 10 minutes. Take it out and make balls out of it and refrigerate for 10 minutes more to set it.
- Melt the chocolate and dip the prepared balls with the help of a fork. Place these dipped balls on parchment paper and refrigerate for 15 minutes.

61

# Peanut Butter Fudge

Peanut Butter Fudge is the recipe to go for when you want to give a creamy and rich treat to yourself or your guests. With its delectable taste and health benefits, not just children but also adults are going to love this sweetness!

## Ingredients

- ½ can condensed milk, sweetened
- ⅔ cup peanut butter

## Method

- Line a square baking tray with aluminum foil exceeding the edges and grease with butter.
- Take a large microwave-suitable bowl, add condensed milk and butter in the same. Heat in the microwave for a minute until melted and smooth. Transfer the mixture into a pan immediately and refrigerate it for about 2 hours.
- Cut into small squares and the fudge is ready.

62

# 3-Ingredient Nutella Brownie

Every time I think of nutella, my mouth waters. This is probably one of the best inventions made by humans. It doesn't matter what my mood is – good, bad, cranky: nutella brownies are my go-to indulgence! This is why I decided to make an easy, 3-Ingredient Nutella Brownie to share the happiness with you as well!

## Ingredients

¼ cup nutella

2 eggs

½ cup almond flour

## Method

- Add all the ingredients in a bowl, mix until the batter is smooth. Pour the mixture in a greased baking pan and level the surface with the help of a spatula.
- In an oven preheated at 180°C or 355°F, place the tray and bake for about 15 minutes. Let the brownies cool and set before cutting and serving.

nutella

# Peach Crumble

This decadent dessert is something you should try out if you are looking to make something that is different than the usual. With the sweetness of the peaches and the tanginess of the raspberries, Peach Crumble is a mouth-watering recipe that needs to be attempted!

## Ingredients

- 6–8 pieces canned peach in syrup, sliced
- 150 gm berries of your choice
- 100 gm granola
- 100 gm coconut cream

## Method

- In a small heated saucepan, pour peaches with syrup on medium flame. Let it simmer until the peaches are hot. Then add raspberries and cook for 2 minutes.
- Put the mixture in serving dishes and top it up with granola and cream.

64

# French Hot Chocolate

Cosy movie nights call for a piping hot cup of French Hot Chocolate! Here is how you can make your own cup of thick chocolate milk.

## Ingredients

100 gm bitter-sweet chocolate, finely chopped

2 cups almond milk

Light brown sugar

Whipped cream (optional)

## Method

- In a pan, heat milk on low flame until warm. Then add chopped chocolate. Stir and melt the chocolate.
- Pour the milk in a serving glass and add the melted chocolate. Add sugar as required.

65

# Baked Custard

I remember as a kid, my mother would frequently serve us this delicious dessert that tastes like heaven. Every time she would ask what I wanted for dessert, I would yell, 'custard'! Eventually, as I myself got into cooking, I realized that I could recreate the same dish with my own specifications! Here is the recipe that I have come to love over the years!

## Ingredients

- 2½ cups milk
- ½ cup coconut sugar
- 4 eggs
- 1 tsp vanilla extract
- A pinch of ground nutmeg

## Method

- Heat milk in a saucepan over medium flame until it nearly comes to boil.
- Meanwhile, in a bowl, take sugar, eggs and vanilla, and whisk the mixture. Add the milk gradually while whisking.
- Preheat an oven to 180°C or 355°F, lightly oil a 1.25-litre baking tray. Pour the mixture in the tray and sprinkle nutmeg.
- Take another larger baking tray and line a tea towel in the same. Place the tray with batter on the tea towel and pour boiling water enough to reach halfway of the batter tray. Bake for 30 minutes.
- Carefully take it out, slice and serve. You may serve it warm or at room temperature or even chilled.

You know those aesthetically pleasing cakes that give you just as much joy when you are cooking them? Marble Cake is one of those cakes that will enamour you even when you are preparing for it.

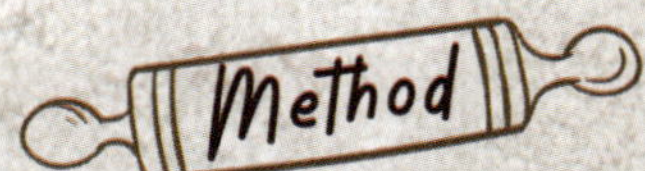


- In a bowl, take butter and sugar. Beat together until lightly fluffy. Gradually beat the milk and also add flour in the bowl. Fold gently.
- Divide this batter into half and add the flour in one and cocoa in the other half of the batter. Place in alternate spoonfuls in a greased and lined 8-inch cake tin.
- Bake for 180°C or 355°F for 20–25 minutes. Take out and let it cool at room temperature.

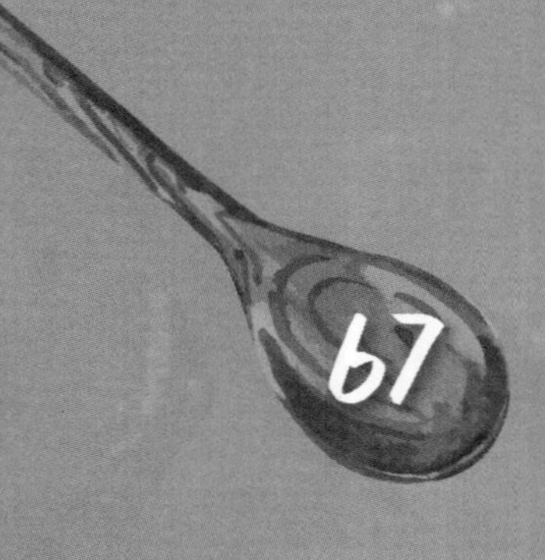

67

# Easy Chocolate Chip Mug Cake

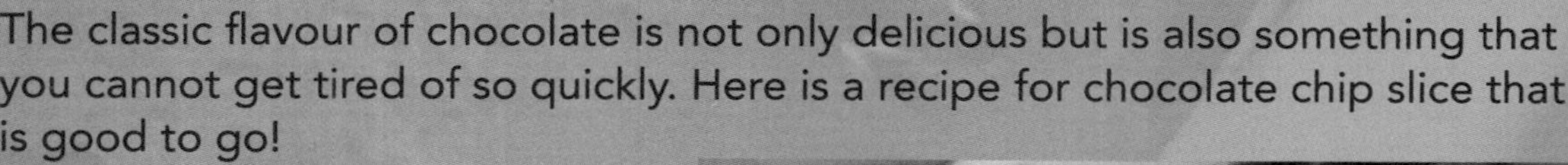

The classic flavour of chocolate is not only delicious but is also something that you cannot get tired of so quickly. Here is a recipe for chocolate chip slice that is good to go!

## Ingredients

- 1 cup cocoa powder
- 1 cup coconut powder
- ¾ cup demerara sugar
- ¾ cup milk
- ¾ cup choco chips

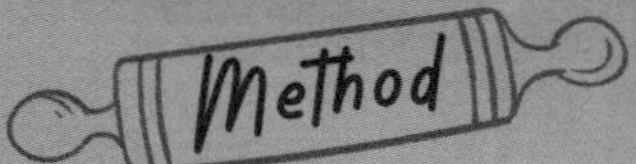

## Method

- Take all the ingredients in a bowl. Mix well. Line a microwave-safe pan with baking paper and spread the mixture over the pan.
- Bake at 180°C or 355°F for approximately 35 minutes. Allow it to cool for 10 minutes. Cut and serve.

68

# Simple Choco Chip Cookies

If cooking therapy wasn't a thing before, I would say make it a little project of yours! Cooking Choco Chip Cookies is the most wholesome experience because the result is so satisfying! Here is my recipe that you can incorporate into your Sunday routine, so that you can have an unlimited access to them throughout the week!

## Ingredients

2 cups milk chocolate chips
2 cups oats flour
1 cup butter
1 cup brown sugar
A pinch of salt
¼ tsp baking powder
½ tsp vanilla extract
2 eggs

## Method

- In a mixing bowl add flour, baking powder, sugar and choco chips and stir. In another bowl take eggs, brown sugar, vanilla and butter, and blend until the colour turns golden. Mix both the mixtures together.
- Give the desired cookie shape and transfer in a baking tray lined with butter paper. Bake for 22–24 minutes in an oven preheated at 160°C or 320°F.

# Bread and Butter Pudding

Incredibly easy and unbelievably delicious, this Bread and Butter Pudding is a classic. With a hint of cinnamon, I find myself preparing this pudding every other day. As I have perfected it, I believe it is worth giving a try!

## Ingredients

300 ml cream
1 tbsp ground cinnamon
40 gm butter, softened
8 slices oats bread, crusts removed
3 eggs
3 tbsp coconut sugar
Handful of raisins

## Method

- Take a slice of bread, spread it with butter and sprinkle a bit of cinnamon.
- Grease an oven-proof dish and place the bread on the dish after cutting the breads in triangles.
- In a bowl, whisk sugar, cream and egg together, pour on the breads, add raisins and bake for 25 minutes in an oven preheated at 200°C or 390°F.

70

# My Delicious Scones

My high tea lovers! You know scones are an essential when it comes to hosting a high tea event. Here is a recipe for you to quickly whip up a delicious batch for when you want to bake a simple dessert without hang-ups!

## Ingredients

½ cup plain flour
2 cups oats flour
1 cup milk
1 cup coconut cream
2 tbsp raisins
1 tsp baking powder

## Method

- Put flour, milk and cream in a bowl and mix them. Fold in the raisins. Transfer this mixture on a board dusted with flour.
- Divide the dough into ten equal parts.
- Shape it into a rough ball and then place the scones in an oven and bake for 20 minutes in an oven preheated at 200°C or 390°F.

**Note**

Refrigerate for 15 minutes before baking and 15 minutes after for best scones.

71

# Banana Bread

Here is the recipe for the bread that stole so many hearts during the pandemic! Everywhere I saw people were cooking up batches of banana bread on the weekends. So, I decided to give it a touch of my own! With a dash of oil, this Banana Bread becomes safe for heart patients to eat without guilt!

## Ingredients

2 cups oats flour
½ cup almond flour
¾ cup brown sugar
1 cup milk
2 tbsp olive oil
1 tsp vanilla essence
1 tsp baking powder
½ tsp baking soda
3 bananas mashed

## Method

- In a bowl, take milk, oil, vanilla, mashed bananas, dry ingredients and sugar. Mix everything well until no lumps are formed.
- Pour the mixture in a greased pan and bake for 30–40 minutes in an oven preheated at 180°C or 355°F.

# Apple Cake

Not the first choice for many, but I love apples! Coming from Shimla, I had access to the freshest, juiciest apples and I made the most of it! When I was living in Shimla, I would constantly experiment with recipes and this is an Apple Cake recipe that I came up with to commemorate my love for this delicious and uber healthy fruit!

## Ingredients

150 gm butter, melted
2 cups oats flour
1 tsp baking powder
½ tsp baking soda
2 cups stewed apple
1 cup brown sugar
½ cup mixed nuts, chopped
2 eggs
2 tsp ground cinnamon

## Method

- Pour all the ingredients in a bowl, mix well. Transfer the mixture in a spring form tin and bake for 40–45 minutes at 140°C or 285°F.
- Enjoy the Apple Cake with friends and family!

# 73 Eggless Banana Sponge

Yet another banana recipe so that you not only make the most out of the goodness of bananas but also enjoy the process of baking even more. This is an easy recipe that you can cook on the weekends when you can spare some quality time to yourself.

## Method

- Mix butter and sugar together. Stir in the mashed bananas and add to the mixture. Heat milk in a microwave for 30 seconds and then add baking soda and stir. Add milk in the mixture and mix well. Sift flour and baking powder, then stir into the mixture.
- Take a greased pan and transfer the mixture in the same. Bake for 20 minutes in an oven preheated at 180°C or 355°F. Allow to cool then layer it with icing sugar and garnish with dry fruits of your choice.

## Ingredients

2 bananas, mashed
1 cup plain flour
125 gm butter
¾ cup sugar
2 tbsp milk
1 tsp baking soda
1 tsp baking powder
Garnish with dry fruits

One of my favourite desserts are tarts. When tart and salted caramel are combined, it leads to only one thing – total deliciousness!

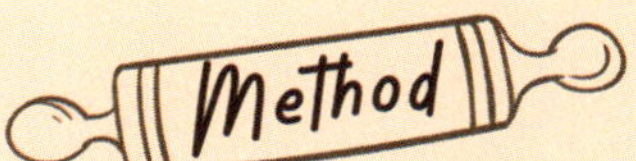


For the tart shells

- Mix flour and butter add a little chilled water, and form a dough; gently knead it with hands.
- Chill for 30 minutes in the fridge.
- Now roll the dough with a rolling pin to 1-inch thinness and spread it evenly on the tart moulds, pressing it up to the edges.
- Cut the excess dough, if any, with a knife or hands making the edges clean.
- Bake at 180°C or 355°F for 5 minutes.
- Take it out and let it cool at room temperature.
- Take caramel spread in a container and microwave for 30 seconds. Place tart shells in a tray and transfer melted caramel in the shell. Fill up two-thirds of the shells. Refrigerate for 20 minutes. Melt the dark chocolate by heating in a microwave and pour it on the tarts. Refrigerate them again until the chocolate sets. Sprinkle sea salt and serve.

75

# Peanut Butter Cups

Do you remember when I introduced to you an easy way of making peanut butter cups? Here is a healthier version of the same! Peanut Butter Cups have always been my go-to dessert whenever I am craving a sweet something. What better way of making the same with a bite of health and deliciousness?

## Ingredients

1½ cups dark chocolate

½ cup natural peanut butter

¼ cup honey

2 tbsp coconut oil

## Method

- In a bowl, add dark chocolate and coconut oil. Microwave until melted, and keep stirring at intervals.
- Line a muffin tin with muffin tin liners and pour half of the mixture in the same. Freeze for 15 minutes.
- In a bowl, take peanut butter, honey and coconut oil and microwave till slightly melted.
- Pour the mixture into the muffin tin and refrigerate for 5 minutes. Pour the rest of the chocolate on top. Refrigerate to set and serve.

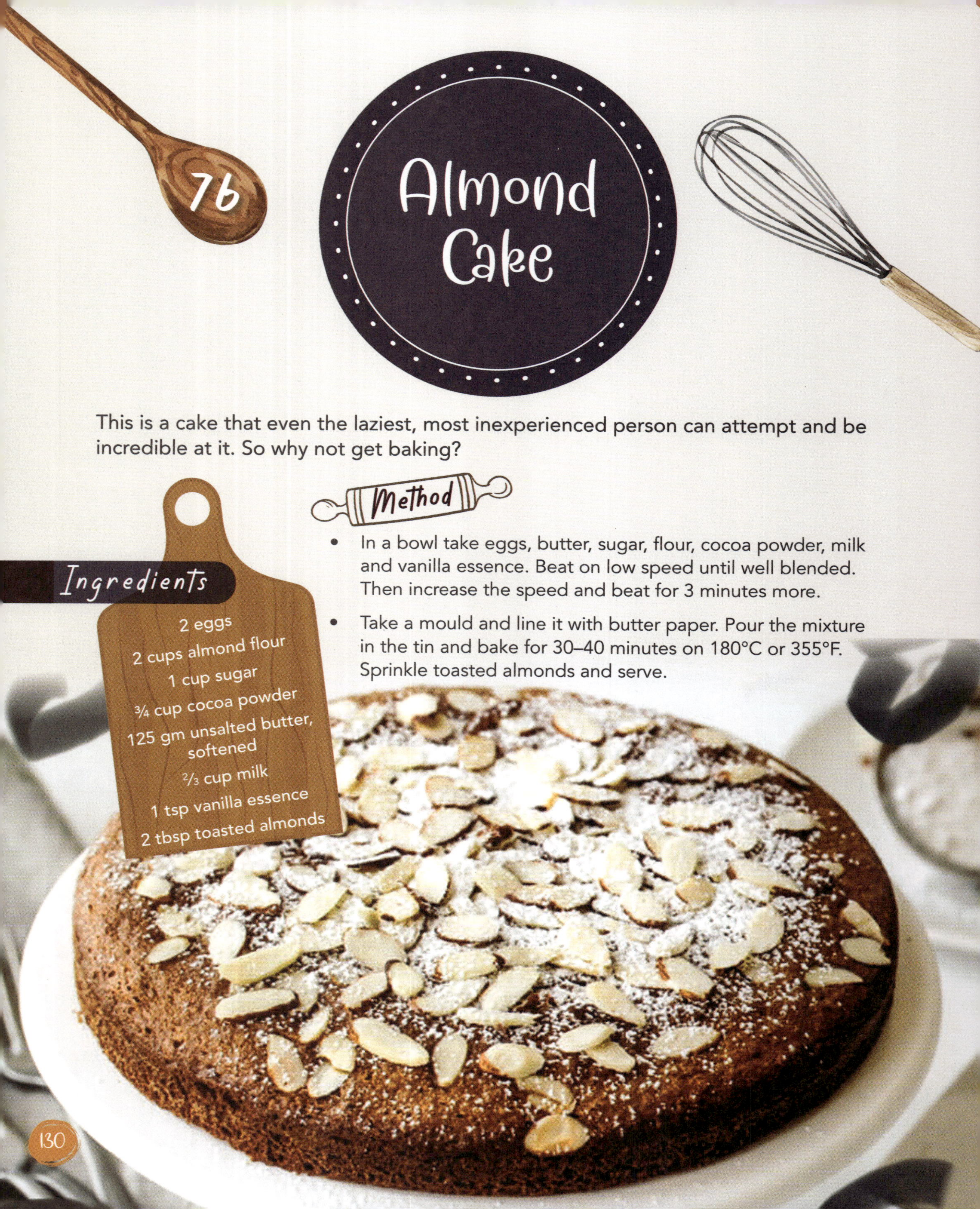

76

# Almond Cake

This is a cake that even the laziest, most inexperienced person can attempt and be incredible at it. So why not get baking?

## Ingredients

2 eggs
2 cups almond flour
1 cup sugar
¾ cup cocoa powder
125 gm unsalted butter, softened
⅔ cup milk
1 tsp vanilla essence
2 tbsp toasted almonds

## Method

- In a bowl take eggs, butter, sugar, flour, cocoa powder, milk and vanilla essence. Beat on low speed until well blended. Then increase the speed and beat for 3 minutes more.
- Take a mould and line it with butter paper. Pour the mixture in the tin and bake for 30–40 minutes on 180°C or 355°F. Sprinkle toasted almonds and serve.

77

# Banana Muffins

One trend I have noticed is that we tend to buy a lot more bananas than we can eat. So instead of throwing away these bananas, why don't we put them to better use and make a batch of go-to sweet snacks?

## Ingredients

2 cups coconut flour
1 cup sugar
4 bananas ripe
1 egg
2 tbsp butter
2 tbsp milk
A pinch of salt

## Method

- Beat egg and bananas together in a bowl. Then add sugar, butter, flour, milk and salt.
- Transfer the mixture into the muffin tins. Bake for 20 minutes in an oven, preheated at 180°C or 355°F.

# Date Loaf

This one is for the fans of dates. You can make a healthy loaf of bread filled with the nutrition and sweetness of dates!

## Ingredients

1 cup boiling water
1 cup dates, chopped
1 cup flour
1 tsp baking powder
1 tsp baking soda
1 egg, beaten
3 tbsp butter

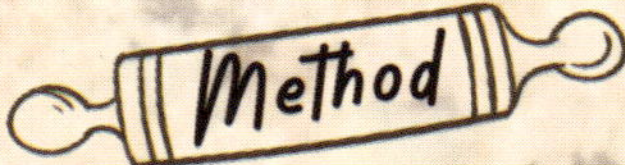

## Method

- In a bowl, mix butter, baking soda, baking powder, boiling water and dates. Mix together and let it rest for 5 minutes. Add flour and egg to the mixture and mix well. Pour into a greased and floured loaf tin.
- Bake for 30–40 minutes in the oven preheated at 160°C or 320°F.

# 79 Coffee Cake

This one is for coffee fanatics. I know that I need a strong cup of coffee to wake up and start functioning like a normal human being. This is a recipe for those who get a heady feeling with the flavour of coffee!

## Ingredients

- 125 gm butter
- 6 tbsp sugar
- ¾ cup flour
- 1/3 cup cream
- 3 eggs lightly beaten
- 1 tsp vanilla essence
- 3 tbsp instant coffee powder
- 1 tbsp warm water

## Method

- In a bowl, beat coffee and sugar until creamy. Add eggs. Add flour and the rest of the ingredients.
- Stir until combined.
- Prepare a baking tin by greasing and line it with butter paper.
- Transfer the mixture in the prepared tin and level the surface.
- Bake in the oven preheated at 160°C or 320°F for 30–40 minutes.

# Assorted Donuts

Now who doesn't like donuts? Biting into these delicious and decadent pieces is like tasting heaven. If you are someone who likes to bake, I suggest you try this recipe out. It is a little tedious and a little tricky but I promise you that the results will be worth the struggle!

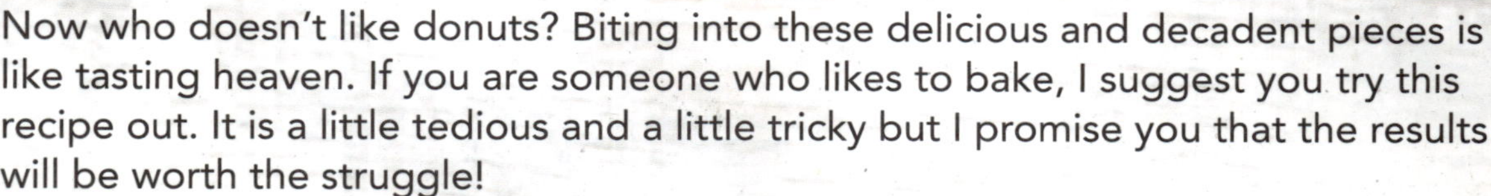

## Method

- In a bowl take warm milk, egg and sugar and whisk well.
- Add yeast, whisk and cover the mixture.
- Let it rest for 5 minutes.
- In a bowl, sift flour, add salt in the same and mix well.
- Now add the yeast mixture and mix.
- Add butter, transfer on a dusted board and knead for about 10–15 minutes.
- Dough should be smooth and stretchy.
- Place the dough in a greased bowl, grease the dough, cover and let it rest for an hour. Take out on a board, knead and knock out the air. Divide in equal parts, roll and shape with donut cutter.
- Place on a prepared baking tray.
- Let the donuts rest for about 20 minutes and then deep-fry until golden brown.
- The donuts are ready, top up with your favourite topping and serve.

## Ingredients

3½ cup flour
250 ml warm milk
50 gm butter, softened
1 egg
2 tbsp sugar
2 tbsp yeast
Oil for frying

81

# Cranberry and Almond Muffins

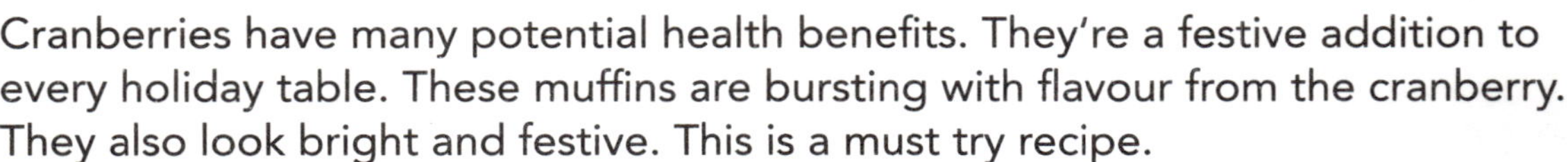

Cranberries have many potential health benefits. They're a festive addition to every holiday table. These muffins are bursting with flavour from the cranberry. They also look bright and festive. This is a must try recipe.

## Method

- In a bowl, take milk, sugar, eggs and salt. Whisk well.
- Add vanilla essence and mix. Add melted butter, whisk and add almond, followed by cranberries.
- Mix well. Sift flour and mix it well.
- Transfer in cupcake moulds placed on a cupcake tray and top up with almond and cranberries.
- Bake in a preheated oven at 180°C or 355°F for about 35–40 minutes.

## Ingredients

250 gm flour
150 ml milk
150 gm sugar
150 gm butter, melted
100 gm cranberries
60 gm almonds, slivered
3 eggs
1 tsp vanilla essence
Salt for taste

# Chocolate Date Nut Bars

If you are a health freak this chocolate-covered nut bars are the perfect answer to your inner fitness influencer. Beautifully structured, you can store this chocolate-covered date nut bars for a long time, although staying away from them will be a challenge in itself!

## Ingredients

- 1 cup dates, pitted and soaked for 30 minutes and drained
- 1½ cups mixed nuts, chopped
- 1 cup dark chocolate chips, melted

## Method

- Take drained dates and nuts in a food processor. Process until dates and nuts are broken and only small chunks of nuts are visible. Mixture should be sticky.
- Now, prepare a baking pan by lining it with parchment paper. Transfer the date mixture in the pan. Press it evenly. Spread melted chocolate on it. Place the pan in refrigerator for 20 minutes then take it out. Cut in bars and serve.

83

# Vanilla Banana Ice Cream

There was a time when I was seriously considering a vegan diet. The biggest drawback I saw was that I would have to give up my beloved ice cream. After all ice cream is a milk-based product! So here is a way you can make a vegan ice cream. You know all those bananas that you end up buying but never using? Just toss them in a freezer and later blend them. Believe it or not, it tastes exactly like an ice cream!

## Ingredients

3 bananas, cut and frozen

¼ cup almond milk

1 tsp vanilla essence

## Method

- Add banana, almond milk and vanilla essence in a food processor and blend it well.
- Transfer the mixture in a bowl and refrigerate. Serve it chilled!

84

# Flourless Sweet Potato Brownies

Here is another recipe for those of you who wish to experiment with veganism! This brownie recipe has a unique twist: it is made of sweet potatoes! A heady mixture of sweet potatoes and cocoa powder will give you the most decadent vegan brownie you have ever tasted!

## Ingredients

- 1 cup mashed sweet potato
- ½ cup almond butter
- ⅔ cup cocoa powder

- Add all the ingredients in a food processor and blend well.
- Transfer in a pan prepared by greasing butter. Bake for 12–15 minutes in an oven preheated at 180°C or 355°F.
- Your sweet potato brownie is ready!

85

# Energy Bites

Here is a recipe for what is probably the healthiest version amongst the brownie recipes. What also helps is that this is a no-bake recipe, i.e., something you can whip up in all of 10 minutes!

## Ingredients

1 cup walnuts
1 cup pitted dates
¼ cup raw cocoa powder
1 tbsp maple syrup

## Method

- Blend walnuts, pitted dates, cocoa powder and maple syrup in a blender. Roll the mixture in balls and serve.

86

# Fresh Fruit Frozen Yogurt

Fresh fruit yogurt is a delicious recipe. Combining yogurt and fruit could provide probiotics, prebiotics, high-quality protein, important fatty acids, and a mixture of vitamins and minerals that have the potential to exert synergistic effects on one's health.

## Ingredients

1 kg yogurt/curd
1–2 bananas, freeze it a night before
3–4 mangoes, freeze it a night before
2 tbsp honey
1 tbsp brown sugar powder
¼ tsp vanilla essence
1 tbsp toasted oats and strawberries for garnish

## Method

- Take a bowl, place a strainer over it along with a cotton cloth. Strain yogurt and keep it hung for 6–8 hours. After 8 hours transfer the yogurt in a bowl. In a food processor take frozen banana, yogurt, brown sugar and vanilla essence. Blend until smooth and refrigerate for 10 hours.
- Similarly, to make frozen mango yogurt, in a food processor, take mango, honey, yogurt and vanilla essence. Blend until smooth and refrigerate for 10 hours before serving.

87

# 5-Ingredient Healthy Brownies

What if I told you that there is a way that you can truly enjoy brownies without feeling too guilty about binging on them? This easy to achieve, 5-ingredient brownie recipe has the goodness of honey and the wholesomeness of whole wheat. This recipe is meant for you to devour guilt-free!

## Ingredients

1 cup dark chocolate, melted
2 eggs
⅓ cup honey
⅓ cup whole wheat flour
¼ cup butter (melted)

## Method

- In a bowl, take eggs and beat until foamy. Add honey, butter, melted chocolate and mix well. Now add flour.
- Fold with the help of spatula.
- Pour the mixture in a greased baking pan.
- Bake for 15 minutes in an oven preheated at 180°C or 355°F.

# 88

# Oats Truffles

Highly nutritious recipe with lots of fibre, beta-glucan, which helps in reducing LDL and total cholesterol. Since it is high in protein and maintains the blood sugar level, it is a very healthy and delicious recipe.

## Ingredients

¾ cup oats
½ cup dark chocolate
¼ cup grated coconut
2 tbsp butter
2 tbsp cocoa powder
2 tbsp honey
1 tbsp almonds

## Method

- In a bowl, add oats, cocoa powder, coconut and almonds. Mix well. In a heated pan take butter and chocolate. Let it melt and mix well.
- Add the melted chocolate and butter in the dry ingredients along with honey. Mix well and make a dough-like mixture. Give desired shape and your Oats Truffles are ready.

# Banana and Cinnamon Ice Cream

A mouth-watering, tempting and fruity dish with a touch of cinnamon is all you need to change your mood when you are on your lows. Because happiness is just a scoop of ice cream.

## Ingredients

2 cup frozen banana, chopped
1½ cup milk
2 tbsp condensed milk
1 tbsp cinnamon powder

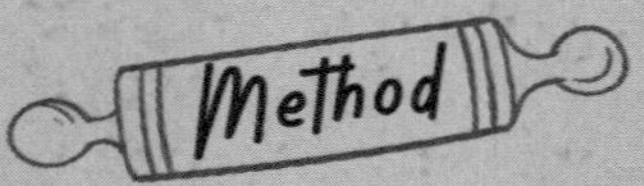

## Method

- In a vessel, take some milk and start stirring in low/medium flame. Add condensed milk and sugar to the same. Cook until thick and reduced. Make sure you do not forget to stir. Once reduced, take it off the flame and let it cool in room temperature.
- In a food processor take banana, grate the cinnamon stick directly into the food processor. Add the reduced milk and blend until smooth.
- Refrigerate it overnight. Your banana ice cream is ready to be relished!

# 90 Oats Crepes

Oats Crepes are a delicious replacement for pancakes. This crepes recipe is perfect because it offers all the nutrition of oatmeal and makes it a complete meal. It can be enjoyed by everyone from kids to elders.

## Ingredients

2 eggs
2 cups ground oats
½ cup milk
½ cup water
1 tsp corn starch
A pinch of salt
2 tbsp olive oil
2 tbsp jam
2 tbsp ground walnuts

## Method

- In a bowl, take eggs and beat well, then sift ground oats followed by corn starch and salt. Whisk well.
- Gradually add milk and water while whisking.
- Let it rest for half an hour in the refrigerator.
- Then grease a heated pan with oil and put the oats batter on the pan keeping the flame medium high.
- Cook for about a minute and flip. Cook for about half a minute more.
- Transfer it on a plate and apply jam over it.
- Spread some grounded nuts. Roll and enjoy!

# Coconut Flour Pancake

This super wholesome recipe will keep you full and satiated for hours. Pancakes are fluffy, cakey, sweet and delicious, and they also contain protein, fibre and healthy fats, with no added sugar, gluten or dairy. This is a perfect recipe for both young and old.

## Ingredients

¼ cup coconut flour
3 eggs
2 tbsp olive oil
2 tbsp maple syrup
1 tsp baking powder
1 tsp vanilla essence
A pinch of salt

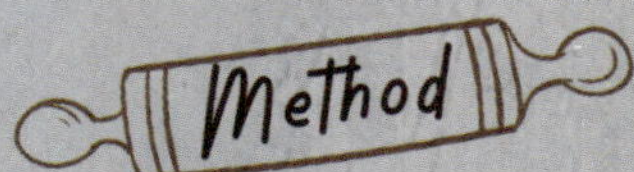

## Method

- Take coconut flour in a bowl, add eggs, oil, maple syrup, baking powder, vanilla essence and salt. Whisk well.
- In the heated pan, add a little oil and pour pancake batter in the pan.
- Once the bottom side is golden brown, flip it and cook on low-medium heat.
- Pancakes are ready.
- Serve them warm with your favourite toppings.

# Almond and Date Bites

Almond and Date Bites are a healthy snack. Made with almonds and dates, it has zero oil content, it will fire up your metabolism, stabilize your blood sugar and, not to forget, will give you guiltless pleasure. This incredibly versatile snack is a must try.

## Ingredients

250 gm dates, deseeded
1 tbsp butter
1 cup desiccated coconut
1 cup almonds

## Method

- Place the dates in a food processor and roughly blend. Take some ghee in a heated pan, add almonds and roast for 5 minutes on low flame. Crush the roasted almonds.
- In the same pan, take some butter and transfer the date purée into the pan. Cook until it softens a bit and add crushed almonds. Add desiccated coconut and mix until well combined.
- Shape the mixture as you like while it's warm. Dip in dry coconut and serve.

Along with its amazing texture and taste, it also has the goodness of berries and nuts.

## Ingredients

3 cups popped rajgira (amaranth)
1 litre milk
¾ cup milk powder
½ cup jaggery
½ tsp cardamom powder
½ tsp nutmeg powder
3 tbsp dry fruit powder

## Method

- In a heated pan, add rajgira and roast on a low flame. Add milk to the same.
- Milk should be hot when you add it on the roasted rajgira.
- Stir and add jaggery and dry fruit powder.
- Bring it to boil and then turn the flame off. Add cardamom and nutmeg powder. Stir. Your Amarnath Kheer is ready to serve.

94

# Almond Flour Chocolate Cake

Rich, moist and spongy, Almond Flour Chocolate Cake is bound to impress, even as it melts in your mouth. A super delicious cake will win over everyone's heart as this wholesome dish is made from a handful of ingredients.

## Ingredients

1 cup almond flour
1 cup brown sugar
½ cup cocoa powder, sifted
4 eggs
1 tbsp plain flour
1 tsp baking powder
1 tsp vanilla extract
½ tsp baking soda
½ tsp salt

## Method

- In a bowl, take almond flour, cocoa powder, baking powder, baking soda and salt.
- Mix until well combined.
- In another large bowl, take eggs and vanilla extract; whisk for 2–3 minutes.
- Add sugar, and whisk.
- Gradually add almond flour mixture, and whisk.
- Grease a cake mould with butter and dust with plain flour. Pour cake batter into it and bake in an oven preheated at 180°C or 355°F for 30–35 minutes.

# Almond and Saffron Phirni

It is a scrumptious and stomach-filling dessert made of almonds. Phirni is a traditional delicacy, a perfect blend of almonds cooked with ground rice, sugar and milk. A festive rice and milk Indian dessert infused with delicate flavours of almond and saffron.

## Method

- Soak rice in water for about 20 minutes. Then strain. Take a piece of cloth and spread the rice. Keep aside and let it dry.
- Soak almond and nuts for 15 minutes. Then remove the outer skin of almond. Place almond and nuts in a food processor and blend into a fine paste.
- Once the rice is dried, blend the rice too along with cardamom. In a heated pan, add milk, nut paste, rice and mix well. Keep stirring. Add saffron and sugar and cook until thick.
- Pour in cups and let it set for 30 minutes to an hour. Garnish with dry fruits and saffron. Serve.

96

# Vegan Kheer

This is a recipe brought in especially for my vegan friends. If you are somebody who is experimenting with veganism, I am here to help you.

## Ingredients

1 cup rice
5 cups almond milk
1 cup water
¼ cup brown sugar
½ tsp salt
½ tsp vanilla extract
Dry fruits for garnish

## Method

- Add rice, milk, water, brown sugar and salt in a large pan. Cook until it boils. Stir continuously keeping the heat medium high.
- Once boiled, lower the heat and cook for about 50 minutes. Add vanilla extract and give it a good mix. Garnish with dry fruits and serve.

97

# Hazelnut Butter Truffles

A delectable dessert which is rich in nutrients. Truffles boost an impressive nutrient profile and are high in many important vitamins and minerals. I have always loved this dish and I hope you will love it too.

## Ingredients

1½ cups hazelnut (roasted, deshelled)
2 tbsp cocoa powder
1 tbsp maple syrup
1½ tsp vanilla extract
1 tsp salt
1 cup melted chocolate

## Method

- Place the nuts in a food processor and blend them until it turns into a smooth paste.
- Add cocoa powder and maple syrup in the paste followed by vanilla extract. Add some salt and blend everything together.
- Transfer the mixture in a bowl.
- Take a small lump of the mixture in your hand and make a roll keeping a hazelnut in the centre.
- Refrigerate for about an hour.
- Take the rolls out.
- Dip in melted chocolate and roll in crushed hazelnut. Serve.

98

# Ragi Kheer

Ragi Kheer is a delicious dessert which can be made in a matter of minutes. This kheer tastes rich and creamy and is full of nutrition. A traditional recipe loved by all.

## Ingredients

4 cups milk
2 tbsp ragi (finger millet), soaked for 8 hours
2 tbsp mixed dry fruits, chopped
½ cup jaggery
¼ tsp cardamom powder

## Method

- Drain the soaked ragi and blend it to paste. Take a pan, pour milk in it and bring it to boil. Once the milk starts boiling, add blended ragi in the milk and cook for about 20 minutes more. Keep stirring continuously as you cook ragi. Add jaggery and continue cooking.
- Finally add cardamom powder and dry fruits. Serve it hot!

99

# Gluten-Free Porridge With Goji Berries and Mixed Seeds

Goji berries are rich in nutrients with several health benefits. This healthy and gluten-free recipe is one to be relished at least once.

## Ingredients

1 cup oats
1 cup milk
1 cup fruits, chopped
1½ cups water
2 tbsp dry fruits, chopped
¼ cup jaggery
½ tsp cardamom powder
1 tbsp honey

## Method

- In a pan, take oats and roast them until golden brown. Add water to it and cook and let it blend. Add jaggery and cook until it melts.
- Add cardamom powder. Mix well. Add dry fruits and milk. Garnish with honey and fruits, and serve.

# Gluten-Free Desserts

Let us understand the word gluten first. Gluten is the natural protein found in grain, especially wheat grain. It helps the flour to be stretchy, it has binding or adhesive properties which gives elasticity to the dough. For example, if we add yeast to the dough, the fermentation caused produces carbon dioxide bubbles which get trapped in the gluten and helps the dough to rise. Baking coagulates the gluten which along with the starch stabilizes the bread or cake and gives it its shape or form! In our country, we consume a lot of wheat as a staple diet, so we don't really follow a gluten-free diet but gluten-free diet might help people who have inflammation and autoimmune reactions in their body.

Being on a gluten-free diet doesn't imply that you cannot enjoy those heavenly desserts, especially now when you've got access to all my gluten-free recipes. In fact, there are many ingredients in our country which are native to us and are gluten-free, for example, millets like bajra (pearl millet), jowar (sorghum), ragi (finger millet), kuttu (buckwheat), corn, etc. We can consume them in the form of grains or grind them and use as flour in cakes, biscuits and all other bakery recipes. Just that the recipe would change slightly and of course the taste would differ from those that are made from wheat flour.

So, now my friends who are on a gluten-free diet, don't have to keep themselves away from those mouth-watering sumptuous desserts, as in this section, I'm sharing some of my favourite recipes with you.

## Ingredients

- 1 cup ragi (finger millet) flour
- ½ cup nuts/seeds of choice
- 10–15 dates
- 2 tbsp vanilla extract
- 1 tbsp coconut oil
- 1 cup cashews, soaked
- 1½ tbsp lemon juice
- 1 cup coconut milk
- 1½ tbsp maple syrup
- 2 tbsp fruit powder
- 1 tbsp agar agar
- Garnish with strawberries

- Blend the nuts in a food processor and add ragi flour to it.
- Add dates followed by vanilla extract and coconut oil and blend again.
- Transfer the mixture in a cake tin and press it to the bottom to ensure a firm crust.
- Put soaked cashews, lemon juice, coconut milk, vanilla extract, maple syrup and fruit powder in a food processor.
- Blend together until smooth and creamy.
- In a pan take some water, add agar agar and cook over medium heat.
- Once it thickens, turn the flame off and transfer agar agar into the food processor. Blend until well combined.
- Transfer this mixture into the tin and refrigerate. Serve it chilled!

## Ingredients

2 cups strawberries
2 cups blueberries
2 cups pitted cherries
3 tbsp orange juice

## Method

- In a pan, take strawberries, blueberries and cherries.
- Add orange juice into the same.
- Cook this mixture for 10–12 minutes over medium heat.
- Allow it to cool and serve.

102

# No-Cream Caramel Sauce

## Ingredients

1 cup coconut milk

½ cup coconut sugar

## Method

In a heated pan, take coconut milk and coconut sugar.

- Stir constantly as you cook.
- Cook until it thickens.
- Once the sauce reaches the desired consistency, turn the flame off.
- Strain to get rid of lumps, if any. Serve and enjoy.

103

# Sugar Cookies

## Ingredients

3 tbsp ground chia seeds
3 tbsp peanut butter
3 tbsp coconut sugar
A pinch of salt
1 cup almond flour
1 cup desiccated coconut
1 tsp vanilla extract
2 tbsp dairy free chocolate chips
½ cup water

## Method

- Take chia seeds in a bowl, add water and mix well and let it rest for 10 minutes.
- Add rest of the ingredients in a bowl and mix well.
- Give it a cookie-like shape and place on a baking tray lined with parchment paper.
- Enjoy!

# Vegan and Gluten-Free Donuts

## Ingredients

1½ cups oats
1 cup grated coconut
1 tbsp flax seeds
1 tsp baking soda
1 tsp baking powder
½ cup coconut sugar
1 tsp lemon juice
1 cup coconut milk
Whipped coconut cream
Sprinklers

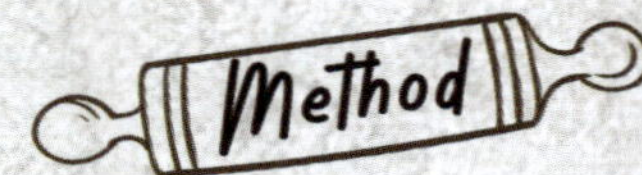

## Method

- In a food processor take oats, coconut, flax seeds, baking soda and baking powder.
- Blend the mixture until fine.
- Transfer the mixture into a large bowl.
- Add coconut sugar, lemon juice and coconut milk into the same.
- Mix until well combined.
- Transfer the mixture into a piping bag.
- Fill the donut moulds with the mixture.
- Bake for 15 minutes at 180°C or 355°F.
- Garnish with whipped coconut cream and some sprinklers. Serve.

## Ingredients

200 gm butter
1 cup sugar
2 eggs
2 cups almond flour
3–4 tbsp of cocoa powder
3–4 tbsp melted chocolate
1 tbsp baking powder
Milk, as required

- Mix butter and sugar in a bowl.
- Add eggs and beat.
- In another bowl, add flour, baking powder and salt.
- Whisk to combine.
- Gradually add the dry ingredients to wet ingredients and milk alternately.
- Whisk to combine.
- Keep one-third of the batter aside.
- In a small cup take cocoa powder.
- Add hot water into the same.
- Whisk until smooth.
- Add this mixture to the one-third batter.
- Add some melted chocolate and mix to combine.
- Spread half of the prepared mixture into a Bundt pan.
- Now transfer the chocolate and cocoa powder mixture and spread it well.
- Add the rest of the mixture on top of the chocolate mixture.
- Bake for an hour.
- Let it cool for 10 minutes. Slice and serve.

106

# Carrot Cake

## Ingredients

**(Cake)**

1 cup carrots, grated

8–10 large good quality dates

¾ cup coconut milk

1 tsp lemon juice

1 tsp vanilla

⅓ cup coconut sugar

1¼ cup bajra (pearl millet) flour

¼ cup tapioca starch

1 tsp baking soda

2 tbsp baking powder

1 tsp cinnamon

¼ tsp ginger powder

**(Cream)**

8 dates

½ cup coconut milk

Lemon juice

4 frozen bananas

## Method

- In a food processor, add grated carrots, dates, milk, lemon juice, vanilla and coconut sugar.

- Grind it all together.
- Further add bajra flour, tapioca starch, baking soda, baking powder, cinnamon, ginger powder, and grind again.
- Transfer this mixture in a cake tin and bake at 180°C or 355°F for 35–40 minutes.
- To prepare the cream, in a food processor, add dates, milk, lemon and banana.
- Blend everything together.
- Once cooled at room temperature, cut the cake into half.
- Place one half of the cake in a tin and spread a layer of cream prepared on top of the cake.
- Repeat the steps once again and garnish with sprinklers.
- Refrigerate overnight. Enjoy.

# 107 Apple Cinnamon Crepes

## Ingredients

- 1 cup ground oats
- 1 cup almond flour
- ½ cup corn starch
- 1½ cups coconut sugar
- ½ cup flax seeds, ground
- 1 tsp baking powder
- 1 large banana
- 2½ cups almond milk
- 1 tsp vanilla extract
- ½ lime juice
- 1½ cups apple (chopped in small cubes)
- 1 tbsp cinnamon
- 2 tbsp peanut butter
- Water as required

## Method

- In a large bowl, take ground oats, almond flour and corn starch, coconut sugar, flax seeds and baking powder.
- Mix until well combined.
- In a blender take banana, milk, vanilla extract and lime juice.
- Blend and transfer on to the dry ingredients.
- Mix well and transfer a ladle full of mixture on a heated pan and cook well on both sides.
- Take apples in a saucepan.
- Add milk into the same followed by corn starch, coconut sugar, cinnamon and lemon juice.
- Mix and cook for 5 minutes.
- Place the stuffing on the prepared crepes and roll.
- To prepare the dressing, take brown sugar and water in a pan.
- Heat until melted.
- Now add some butter into the same and cook for a minute more.
- Drizzle the prepared dressing on crepes and serve.

108

# Chocolate Bars (Vegan)

## Ingredients

1 cup almonds
1 cup fresh coconut
½ cup nut butter
½ cup maple syrup
1 large cup chocolate

## Method

- Take almonds and coconut in a food processor and grind.
- In a saucepan, take butter and maple syrup and cook until it melts.
- Transfer almond and coconut mixture into a bowl and add melted butter and maple syrup.
- Mix and transfer on a rectangular tray lined with butter paper.
- Level the mixture and bake for 8–10 minutes at 180°C or 355°F.
- After baking let it cool and cut them vertically lengthwise to give it a rectangular shape.
- Crumble the cut-off edges of the baked mixture into half of the melted chocolate.
- Take one baked stick and spread this chocolate on the same.
- Make another two such layers and refrigerate for 10–15 minutes.
- Coat it with plain melted chocolate.
- Refrigerate until firm. Enjoy.

109

# S'Mores

## Ingredients

- 2 cups granola
- 1 tbsp baking soda
- 1 tsp cinnamon
- A pinch of salt
- ½ cup coconut flour
- ½ cup almond butter
- ½ cup maple syrup or honey
- 1 tsp vanilla
- Chocolate

## Method

- Take granola in a food processor and grind.
- Add baking soda, cinnamon, salt and flour and grind to mix.
- Further add almond butter, maple syrup or honey, and vanilla, and grind.
- Now transfer this batter into a cupcake tray.
- Press this mixture to the bottom tightly to form a cup-like shape.
- Bake it for 12–15 minutes at 180°C or 355°F or till a toothpick comes clean when poked into the cupcake.
- Garnish with chocolate and serve.

# Chocolate Pie

## Ingredients

1 cup almonds
½ cup cocoa powder
1 tsp salt
3 tbsp coconut oil
8–10 dates
1 cup almond milk
1 unsweetened chocolate bar, melted

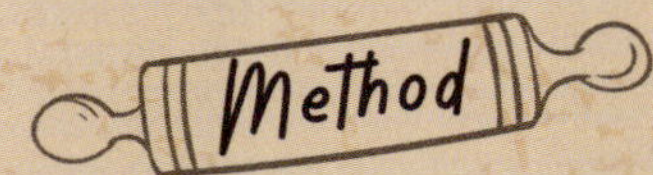

## Method

- In a food processor, take almonds, cocoa powder and salt, and grind.
- Add coconut oil into the same and grind to mix.
- Transfer this mixture into a cake tin and press it down to form crust.
- Refrigerate.
- Now, take dates, almond milk and unsweetened chocolate into a blender and blend it smooth.
- Transfer this mixture into the tin. Refrigerate overnight and enjoy.

# Cherry Pie

## Ingredients

1 cup oats flour
1 cup maple syrup or date syrup
¼ cup coconut oil
1 tsp salt
2 cups cherries, frozen
½ cup corn starch
1 tbsp vanilla extract
Handful of oats, crumbled
Scoops of ice cream (optional)

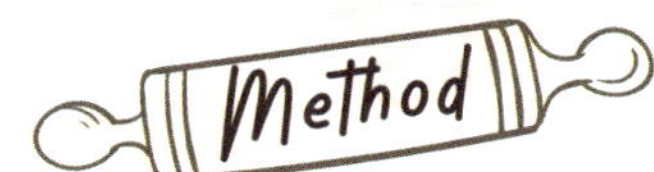


## Method

- In a bowl, take oats flour, maple syrup, coconut oil and salt.
- Mix together until well combined.
- Transfer this mixture into a cake tin and press to form crust.
- Take frozen cherries and add starch, maple syrup or date syrup and vanilla extract into the same.
- Mix well and transfer the mixture into the cake tin.
- Top up with crumbled oats. Bake.
- Serve with a scoop of ice cream.

# Gluten-Free Pumpkin Bars

## Ingredients

- 1 cup pumpkin, boiled and mashed
- 1 tbsp baking soda
- 1 tbsp baking powder
- 1 tsp salt
- 1 tbsp ground cinnamon
- 1 tsp garam masala powder
- 2 tsp pure vanilla extract
- 1½ cups brown sugar
- 3 eggs
- 2 cups coconut flour
- 1 cup vegetable oil

## Method

- In a bowl, take pumpkin, baking soda, baking powder, salt, cinnamon, spice and vanilla extract.
- Mix well and add brown sugar.
- Mix and add eggs.
- Add gluten-free flour and vegetable oil, and mix well.
- Transfer the mixture in a greased tray and bake for 25–30 minutes at 180°C or 355°F.
- Once cooled, cut into bars and serve.

113

# Snickerdoodle Peanut Butter Cookies

## Ingredients

100 gm peanut butter
1 cup granulated sugar
1 tbsp pure vanilla extract
2 eggs
2–3 tbsp cream
1 tsp baking soda
1 tsp salt
2 cups gluten-free flour
2 tbsp cinnamon

## Method

- In a bowl take butter and sugar.
- Beat well.
- Add vanilla extract, cream and eggs; beat again.
- Beat in baking soda and salt.
- Add flour and mix well.
- Shape the cookies and roll into cinnamon and sugar mixture.
- Bake and serve.

114

# Gluten-Free Ragi Cupcakes

## Ingredients

- ¾ cup ragi flour
- ½ cup oats ground to powder
- 1 tsp baking powder
- 1 tsp baking soda
- ½ cup cocoa powder
- ½ cup sugar
- 3 eggs
- ½ cup milk
- ½ cup melted butter
- 1 tsp vanilla essence
- Water as required

## Method

- Take a bowl and mix the ragi flour, oats powder, baking powder, baking soda and cocoa powder.
- Then beat the eggs and sugar. Finally add the melted butter, vanilla essence and milk. Mix all the ingredients well.
- Pour this batter into cupcake moulds. Put it at 160°C or 320°F for 30 mins and bake it.
- Enjoy these delicious cupcakes as it is or top it up with your favourite topping to add that extra flavour.

# Vegan Desserts

Veganism, which is the practice of abstaining from using or consuming any animal products or by-products, is becoming increasingly popular around the world. More humane, more considerate of our world and its various species, certainly kinder and with myriad health and other far-reaching benefits, veganism is a strong philosophy in both belief and practice.

However, when one loves to cook and especially bake or make sweet things, how limiting is veganism? If you cannot use butter or cheese or any milk products, eggs, or honey, does it mean that you must sacrifice cooking up or relishing your favourite desserts? Does that mean you have to compromise on the taste or flavour or yumminess? In this section, we firmly establish that being a practising vegan and wanting to avoid consuming animal products in no way stop you from satiating your sweet tooth! And vegan alternatives don't have to be super expensive or difficult to find either.

From the most gorgeous Cinnamon Rolls to a rich Rum Cake and from Chocolate Sesame Cookies and Blueberry Millet Tarts to refreshingly light Panna Cotta, I take you through some luscious dessert recipes which are 100 per cent vegan and also super delicious!

So, now you can have your cake and eat it too – without compromising on your health, happiness or belief system. Dig into these divinely different recipes and enjoy your foray into whipping up some of the best vegan dessert treats!

# Vegan Chocolate Sesame Cookies

## Ingredients

1 cup almond
½ cup tahini
Dairy-free chocolate, melted
5 tbsp date syrup
1 tbsp flax seeds
¼ tsp baking powder
A pinch of salt
Sesame seeds

## Method

- Preheat an oven to 180°C or 355°F.
- Grind almonds and flax seeds.
- In a bowl, take tahini, almonds, flax seeds, baking powder, salt and maple syrup.
- Mix well. Roll the mixture into balls and press to give a cookie-like shape.
- Now roll the prepared cookies in sesame seeds.
- Refrigerate for about 15 minutes.
- Now, place the cookies in the preheated oven and bake for 8–10 minutes.
- Let the cookies cool down.
- Enjoy with a cup of soy milk.

116

# Vegan Hot Chocolate

## Ingredients

- 2 cups almond milk
- 50 gm dairy-free chocolate bar, chopped
- 2 tbsp cocoa powder
- 1 tbsp coconut sugar
- ½ tsp corn starch

## Method

- In a saucepan take cocoa powder and corn starch.
- Mix and add almond milk into the same.
- Cook until it thickens, then add coconut sugar and chocolate into the same.
- Stir and cook until the chocolate melts. Enjoy.

117

# Vegan Fudge

## Ingredients

3 cups full-fat coconut milk
2 cups chocolate chips (dairy-free)
3 tbsp almond butter
½ cup date syrup

## Method

- Place the chocolate in a saucepan, melt it over low heat stirring continuously.
- Now add the rest of the ingredients and stir until well combined.
- Transfer the mixture in a tray lined with parchment paper and refrigerate until it sets. Enjoy.

118

# Vegan Pancake

## Ingredients

2 cups flour
2 tbsp coconut sugar
2 tsp baking powder
½ tsp salt
2 cups almond milk
2 tbsp apple cider vinegar
2 tbsp peanut butter
2 tsp vanilla
Maple syrup and fresh fruit (garnish)

## Method

- Add apple cider vinegar and vanilla in almond milk.
- Mix and let it sit for 5–7 minutes.
- Meanwhile, in a bowl take flour, sugar, baking powder and salt.
- Mix all the ingredients.
- Now add the prepared milk into the dry ingredients and whisk.
- Now let it rest for about 5 minutes.
- Transfer a ladle full of prepared batter on a heated and greased pan.
- Cook from both sides until golden brown and serve with fresh fruit and maple syrup.

119

# Vegan Cheesecake

## Method

- In a food processor, take almonds, dates and shredded coconut and blend.
- Transfer this mixture into a cake tin and press it to the bottom to make it firm and even.
- Let it chill in the fridge for 30 minutes.
- Now put cashews, maple syrup, unsweetened cocoa powder, coconut butter and coconut milk in a food processor.
- Blend until it is smooth and creamy.
- Transfer this mixture on top of the crust.
- Refrigerate for at least 3 hours. Serve it chilled.

## Ingredients

1 cup almonds
10–15 dates, de-seeded
1 cup coconut, shredded
1½ cups cashews, soaked overnight
½ cup maple syrup
½ cup unsweetened cocoa powder
2 tbsp coconut butter
1 cup coconut milk

## Ingredients

**(For cake)**

350 gm coconut flour
250 ml almond milk
200 gm organic brown sugar
200 ml olive oil
120 ml honey
2½ tsp baking powder
2½ tsp ground ginger
1½ tsp pure vanilla extract
1 tsp ground cinnamon
¾ tsp ground nutmeg
½ tsp baking soda
½ tsp fine sea salt
½ tsp ground allspice
¼ tsp ground cloves

**(For pomegranate glaze)**

250 gm powdered sugar
4 tbsp pomegranate juice
1 tbsp lemon juice

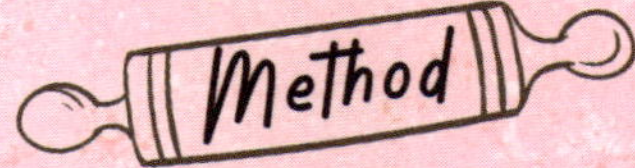


**Cake**

- Preheat the oven to 140°C or 340°F.
- Grease a cake mould with oil and sprinkle with flour.
- In a large bowl, sift flour, baking powder, baking soda, salt, ginger, allspice, cinnamon, nutmeg and cloves.
- Mix well.
- Add almond milk, oil, honey, brown sugar and vanilla. Mix all the ingredients with the help of an electric mixer.
- Transfer the mixture into the prepared tin and place it in the middle rack of the oven for 40–45 minutes.
- Allow the cake to cool, then invert it on to a cooling rack.

**Pomegranate glaze**

- Place powdered sugar in a bowl.
- Add lemon juice and pomegranate juice one tbsp at a time, whisking until smooth and thick.
- Make sure the glaze is glossy, sticky but pourable.
- Pour the glaze on the cake and enjoy!

## Ingredients

300 ml water
60 ml coconut milk
60 ml oat milk
50 gm sugar
¼ cup raw cashews, soaked in water for 15 minutes
2 tbsp almond flour
2 tbsp pistachio sliced
2 tbsp mixed dry fruits
7–8 saffron strands
1 green cardamom pod seeds
A pinch of salt

## Method

- Blend coconut milk, oat milk, cashews, pistachio, saffron and seeds of the cardamom pod together.
- Transfer this mixture into a saucepan over medium heat and bring it to boil, stirring occasionally.
- Now, add almond flour, salt and sugar.
- Mix well and cook until the mixture is thickened to preference.
- Turn the heat off and let it cool.
- Transfer in serving bowl.
- Top it up with mixed dry fruits and serve.

# Vegan Rum Cake

## Ingredients

2 tbsp dark raisins
2 tbsp dried cranberries
4–5 dates
4–5 dried figs
2 tsp grated ginger
1 tsp orange zest
1 tsp lemon zest
½ cup granulated sugar
2 tbsp flax seeds
½ tsp baking soda
1 tsp baking powder
1 tsp ground cinnamon
½ tsp ground ginger
¼ tsp cardamom
A pinch of nutmeg
1 cup coconut flour
½ cup olive oil
5 tbsp almond butter
½ cup almonds, chopped
½ cup rum
Egg replacer

## Method

- Cut all dried fruits to the same size as raisins and cranberries. Place in a medium bowl and pour rum over it.
- Microwave for a minute and let it rest for 3–4 hours.
- In a large saucepan, take fruit, zest, ginger, spices, sugar, oil and butter.
- Bring it to boil.
- Reduce heat and let it simmer again for 10 minutes.
- Remove whole spices once cooled.
- Add nuts, sifted flour, egg replacer, baking soda and powder.
- Pour the batter in a greased tin.
- Bake at 180°C or 355°F for 20–25 minutes.
- Let the cake cool, then flip it.
- Wrap and store up to two weeks.

123

# Guava Ice Cream

## Ingredients

5–6 guavas

¼ cup vegan condensed milk

¼ cup dairy-free cream

3 tbsp coconut sugar

## Method

- Peel the guavas and cut roughly.
- Make a fine paste of the guava and strain.
- Now transfer it in the food processor, add milk, cream and sugar into the same.
- Process until everything is well combined.
- Transfer the prepared ice cream in ice cream moulds and refrigerate them overnight.

124

# Vegan Panna Cotta

## Ingredients

500 ml coconut milk
2 tbsp sugar
1 tbsp powdered agar agar
1 vanilla bean

**Topping**

1 cup raspberries
1 tbsp sugar
1 tsp lemon juice
120 ml water

## Method

- Add coconut milk and sugar in a medium-sized saucepan over medium heat.
- Bring it to boil. Then whisk in agar agar.
- Continue boiling for 3 minutes more.
- Add vanilla bean seeds to the mixture and whisk well to combine.
- Pour the mixture into ramekins or small serving glasses and refrigerate for about an hour.
- To prepare the topping, add raspberry, sugar, lemon and water into a saucepan.
- Cook uncovered over medium heat for 10–15 minutes.

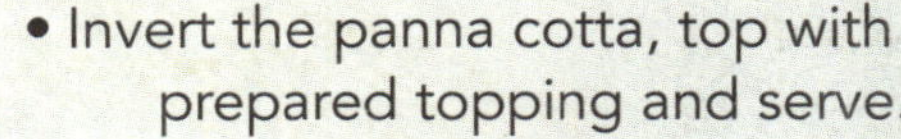

- Invert the panna cotta, top with prepared topping and serve.
- You can also serve in ramekins or glasses.

# Vegan Cinnamon Rolls

## Ingredients

**(Dough)**
4 cups flour
2 cups almond milk, room temperature
½ cup almond butter
¼ cup coconut sugar
1 packet active dry yeast
1 tsp salt

**(Rolls)**
¾ cup vegan butter
1 cup brown sugar
2 tbsp cinnamon

**For the glaze**
1 cup coconut sugar
2 tbsp almond milk
½ tsp vanilla

## Method

- In a large bowl, take milk, butter and sugar, mix and add active dry yeast and let it sit for 5 minutes.
- Now, add flour and salt. Mix everything until well combined.
- Cover and let it rest for an hour.
- Dust some flour on a board, place the dough on the same and knead well.
- Roll it half-inch-thick and brush the rolled dough with vegan butter.
- Spread brown sugar and sprinkle with cinnamon powder.
- Roll and cut. Place in a well-greased tray keeping some distance in between.
- Cover and let the rolls rest for at least 30 minutes.
- Bake at 180°C or 355°F for 25–30 minutes.
- In a bowl take sugar, almond milk and vanilla. Mix well.
- Spread on the prepared cinnamon rolls and serve.

# Vegan Cherry and Almond Brownies

## Ingredients

250 gm caster sugar
100 gm flour
80 gm dairy-free dark chocolate
60 gm vegan margarine
50 gm ground almond
50 gm tinned cherry
50 gm cocoa powder
2 tbsp ground flax seeds
1½ tsp vanilla extract
¼ tsp baking powder
A pinch of salt

## Method

- Heat the oven to 170°C or 340°F.
- Grease and line a cake mould with parchment paper.
- In a cup take flax seeds. Add six tablespoonful water into the same, mix it and keep aside for 5 minutes.
- In a saucepan, take chocolate and margarine with 60 ml of water and cook on low heat until melted.
- Allow it to cool. Put flour, almond, cocoa, baking powder and salt in a bowl and stir to remove any lumps.
- Add sugar into the melted chocolate mixture and beat well until smooth.
- Add the cherries in flax seeds mixture, add vanilla extract into the chocolate mixture and combine. Keep adding the flour mixture and stir it well. Transfer the mixture in prepared tin and bake for 35–45 minutes.
- Once done, take it out and let it cool completely.
- Cut in squares and serve. Or store in an airtight container up to three days.

# Pecan Pie Bars

## Ingredients

1 cup pecans
A handful of whole pecans
½ cup shredded coconut
20 dates
1 cup coconut milk
1 tsp vanilla essence
½ tsp sea salt
3 tbsp corn starch

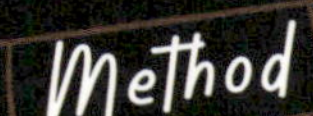

## Method

- In a food processor, take chopped pecans, shredded coconut and dates.
- Make a rough mixture of the ingredients.
- Transfer in a baking tray lined with parchment paper and press tightly to make a strong crust.
- Now, take 8–10 dates, milk, vanilla and starch in a blender and blend until smooth.
- Add whole pecans and blend roughly.
- Transfer this mixture in the tray on top of the prepared crust.
- Level it and top up with some more pecans.
- Bake for 35–40 minutes at 180°C or 355°F. Cut and serve.

# Blueberry Millet Tarts

## Ingredients

**For the crust**

1 cup flour

¼ cup millets (mix of jowar, bajra and ragi in equal parts)

½ cup sugar

8 tbsp butter, cut into small pieces

**For the filling**

3 cups fresh blueberries, rinsed and dried

2 tbsp corn starch

2 tsp lemon zest finely chopped

2 tbsp fresh lemon juice

⅔ cup sugar

A pinch of salt

## Method

- Preheat oven to 180°C or 355°F.
- In a bowl, combine flour, millet flour, sugar and butter. Mix lightly with hands until it looks like bread crumbs.
- Divide the dough into individual tart pans and Press into the tart mould up to the sides until firmly packed. Freeze for 10 minutes. Prick the dough with a fork so that it doesn't rise when baked.
- Now bake for 10–12 minutes at 180°C or 355°F.
- Bring one-third cup water and 2 cups of berries to a boil.
- Now reduce the heat and simmer. Stir occasionally, until berries become slightly soft (approx 5 minutes).
- Now in a small bowl, mix corn starch with two tablespoons water. Stir into the berry mixture.
- Add lemon zest and juice, sugar and salt. Bring to a boil, then reduce heat. Simmer and stir for a minute or until the mixture starts to thicken.
- Remove from flame and keep aside. Let it cool at room temperature.
- Now pour half the berry mixture into two cups of whipped cream and mix until well combined. Transfer it into a piping bag and fill each tart shell with the mix.
- Now garnish each tart shell with fresh blueberries and enjoy!

129

# Vegan Chocolate Avocado Mousse

## Ingredients

- 2 ripe avocados
- ½ cup semi-sweet chocolate chips
- ¼ cup cocoa powder
- ¼ cup brown sugar
- ¼ cup coconut milk
- 1 tbsp vanilla extract
- Agave nectar

## Method

- In a food processor, take two avocados.
- Microwave chocolate chips for about a minute to melt.
- Add the melted chocolate, cocoa powder, coconut milk, vanilla extract, pinch of salt and agave nectar into the food processor.
- Blend until smooth.
- Transfer the mixture into a piping bag with open star tip.
- Spoon it into a serving glass. You can refrigerate it or serve it as it is.

# Acknowledgements

I am delighted to extend my heartfelt gratitude to all those who have contributed to the creation and completion of this delectable journey through the world of desserts. Without your support, passion and encouragement, this cookbook would not have been possible.

First and foremost, I would like to express my deepest appreciation to my family and friends for their unwavering belief in my culinary aspirations. Your continuous encouragement, enthusiasm and willingness to be my taste-testers have been invaluable. Thank you for always being there to inspire and motivate me throughout this entire endeavour.

Special thanks to Rashmi Uday Singh for the foreword, writing amidst a super busy travel schedule and always encouraging, loving and supporting me!

My sincere gratitude to Ajay Mago, publisher Om Books International and Shantanu Ray Chaudhuri, editor-in-chief for believing in my vision and for turning it into a reality. Heartfelt thanks to Sheela Roy, editor, and Sheena Agarwal, designer. Your dedication, professionalism, and meticulous attention to detail have been instrumental in shaping this book into a culinary masterpiece. Last but not the least, a big thank you to Suhail Mathur for his support.

A special acknowledgement goes to the talented chefs, bakers and my team who have influenced and inspired my passion for desserts. I would like to thank Sanjana Santosh, Shurtika Koladia, Sonal, Divyesh Parmar, Ayan and the entire team. Your creativity, innovation and commitment to the art of baking have set the bar high and continue to push the boundaries of what is possible in the realm of sweets.

To my loyal readers and followers, thank you for your unwavering support, feedback and encouragement. Your enthusiasm for my culinary creations and success of *Sinfully Yours* has been a source of inspiration and motivation to come up with *Sinfully Yours: Just Desserts*. I am deeply grateful for your trust and for joining me on yet another sweet adventure.

In conclusion, this cookbook is the culmination of the love, passion and hard work of countless individuals who have all played a part in its creation. To each and every one of you, I extend my sincerest thanks. Your contributions have made this cookbook a reality, and I hope it brings joy, inspiration and a touch of sweetness to the lives of all who turn its pages.

Sinfully yours,

Shipra Khanna

# Index


A

Almond and Date Bites 153

Almond and Saffron Phirni 157

Almond Cake 130

Almond Flour Chocolate Cake 155

Amaranth Kheer with Nuts and Berries 154

Apple Cake 124

Apple Cinnamon Crepes 176

Assorted Donuts 136

B

Baked Chilli Yogurt 99

Baked Custard 115

Banana and Cinnamon Ice Cream 146

Banana Berry Fruit 105

Banana Bread 123

Banana Muffins 131

Banoffee Split 83

Beetroot Halwa 96

Berry Panna Cotta 30

Blueberry Millet Tarts 210

Bread and Butter Pudding 121

C

Carrot Cake 174

Cherry Pie 183

Chocolate Bars (Vegan) 178

Chocolate Coconut Balls 108

Chocolate Cookies 10

Chocolate Date Nut Bars 139

Chocolate Duo Mousse 103

Chocolate Fudge 107

Chocolate Pie 180

Chocolate Walnut Cake 9

Cinnamon and Oats Tea Cake 42

Coconut Flour Pancake 150

Coconut Laddoos 84

Coconut Macaroons 43

Coffee Cake 135

Cranberry and Almond Muffins 138

Crepes 80

Custard Bites 94

D

Date Loaf 132

Devil's Dark Fantasy 17

Dry Fruit Laddoos 79

E

Easy Chocolate Chip Mug Cake 118

Eggless Banana Sponge 125

Eggless Caramel Custard 31

Eggless Chocolate Chip Cookies 36

Eggless Choco Fudge 18

Eggless Low-Fat Tutti Frutti Cake 22

Energy Bites 142

F

5-Ingredient Healthy Brownies 144

Flourless Sweet Potato Brownies 141

French Hot Chocolate 114

Fresh Fruit Frozen Yogurt 143

Fruit Jalebi 61

Fruit Trifle 20

G

Gluten-Free Marble Cake 173

Gluten-Free Porridge.....Mixed Seeds 161

Gluten-Free Pumpkin Bars 185

Gluten-Free Ragi Cupcakes 187

Guava Ice cream 202

Gulab Jamun with Jaggery 47

H

Hazelnut Butter Truffles 159

Healthy Bite on the Go! 82

K

Kaju Katli 58

L
Lauki Halwa 50
Lemon Semifreddo 12
Lemon Tart 33
M
Makhana Pudding 88
Mango Coconut Frozen Yogurt 106
Mango Ice Cream 78
Mango Shrikhand 64
Marble Cake 116
Matcha Tea Cake 32
Microwave Banana Pudding 85
Mini Salted Caramel Tarts 127
Mocha Truffles 75
Modak 55
Moong Dal Halwa 51
My Delicious Scones 122
My Fudgy Brownies 40
N
No-Bake Choco-Walnut Tarts 100
No-Cream Caramel Sauce 168
O
Oats Crepes 148
Oats Cupcakes 29
Oats Truffles 145
1-Minute Microwave Eggless Brownie 74
P
Papaya Halwa 68
Pavlova 15
Payasam 62
Peach Crumble 112
Peanut Butter Cups 72
Peanut Butter Cups (Healthier Version) 128
Peanut Butter Cupcakes 76
Peanut Butter Fudge 109
Peanut Chikki 56
Pecan Pie Bars 208
Pineapple Sandesh 92
Pineapple Sheera 95
Plum Cake 35
Pomegranate and Gingerbread Cake 196
Puran Poli 52
R
Rabri Malpua 63
Ragi Kheer 160
Rava Cake 91
S
Salt Caramel Custard 26
Seviyan Kheer 48
Simple Choco Chip Cookies 119
Sitaphal Rabri 66
S'Mores 179
Snickerdoodle Peanut Butter Cookies 186
Strawberry Banana Coconut Pop 104
Strawberry Cheesecake Vegan Bars 165
Sugar Cookies 169
T
3-Ingredient Nutella Brownie 110
Tiramisu 25
Topping Berry Compote 166
V
Vanilla Banana Ice Cream 140
Vegan and Gluten-Free Donuts 170
Vegan Cherry and Almond Brownies 207
Vegan Cheesecake 195
Vegan Chocolate Avocado Mousse 212
Vegan Chocolate Sesame Cookies 191
Vegan Cinnamon Rolls 204
Vegan Fudge 193
Vegan Hot Chocolate 192
Vegan Kheer 158
Vegan Pancake 194
Vegan Panna Cotta 203
Vegan Rabri 198
Vegan Rum Cake 201
W
Walnut and Fig Pie 39

CREAM
CREAM
CREAM
CREAM
CREAM